Future PLC Quay House, The Ambury, Bath, BA1 1UA

Future Genius Editorial
Content Director **Dr Gemma Lavender**
Editorial Content **Jack Parsons & David Crookes**
Senior Designer **Steve Dacombe**
Head of Art & Design **Greg Whitaker**
Editorial Director, Bookazines **Jon White**
Managing Director **Sarah Rafati Howard**

Contributors
Special thanks to the UK Department of Education
and US Department of Education, Briony Duguid, Thomas
Parrett, Neo Phoenix, Newton Ribeiro, Laurie Newman

Cover Images
Getty Images

Photography
Getty Images, Alamy
All copyrights and trademarks are recognised and respected

Advertising
Media packs are available on request
Commercial Director **Clare Dove**

International
Head of Print Licensing **Rachel Shaw**
licensing@futurenet.com
www.futurecontenthub.com

Circulation
Head of Newstrade **Tim Mathers**

Production
Head of Production **Mark Constance**
Production Project Manager **Matthew Eglinton**
Advertising Production Manager **Joanne Crosby**
Digital Editions Controller **Jason Hudson**
Production Managers **Keely Miller, Nola Cokely,
Vivienne Calvert, Fran Twentyman**

Printed in the UK

Distributed by Marketforce, 5 Churchill Place, Canary Wharf,
London, E14 5HU www.marketforce.co.uk Tel: 0203 787 9001

Future Genius: The World (FGB4674)
© 2022 Future Publishing Limited

FUTURE Connectors.
Creators.
Experience
Makers.

Future plc is a public
company quoted on the
London Stock Exchange
(symbol: FUTR)
www.futureplc.com

Chief executive **Zillah Byng-Thorne**
Non-executive chairman **Richard Huntingford**
Chief financial officer **Penny Ladkin-Brand**

Tel +44 (0)1225 442 244

Widely
Recycled

For press freedom
with responsibility

Future Genius

The World

Discover a whole wide world of wonders with Future Genius. You can learn all about lands close to home and oceans away through fascinating facts, colourful maps, incredible photos and amazing illustrations. Test your knowledge of people, places, animals and environments with puzzles and quizzes. And go further with fun fieldwork projects, such as mapping your neighbourhood, experimenting with a homemade volcano, and creating your own compass. Let's explore!

WHAT'S INSIDE

6   Our Planet

8   Biomes

10   Ecosystems

12   Topography

14   Glaciers

16   Oceans

18   Rivers

20   Islands

22   Mountain ranges

24   Lakes

26   Deserts

30   Planet puzzles

36   The World

38   Africa

42   Asia

46   Central America

50   North America

54   South America

58   Europe

64   The Middle East

68   South East Asia

72   Australia

76   The Arctic

80   The Antarctic

84   World puzzles

88   World activities

98   Fun facts about the world

36

58

84

98

INTERACTIVE EXPERIENCE

 Scan the QR code with your device's camera or download a free QR code reader app. Many iPhone and Android devices include these features

 When you see the "Scan with your phone or tablet" prompt, use your device to scan the QR code, which looks like this

 Hold your mobile device over the image and watch it come to life! Your device needs to be connected to the internet for this to function

OUR PLANET

There's no place like home – and that's a fact. Scientists scanning outer space with satellites and telescopes have found more than 5,000 planets so far. Some are a similar size to Earth or just as rocky. A few have atmospheres and possibly even underground oceans. But our planet is the only one in the whole universe that we know contains life.

From amoeba to elephants and zebrafish to oak trees, our planet has all sorts of plants and animals. So many, in fact, that they've covered the world in forests and grasslands, coral reefs and swamps.

As animals, humans have also transformed Earth. We're constantly building towns, cities and roads, and more recently we've even changed the planet's climate. Part of the reason Earth is such a great place for plants and animals to live is that it's alive itself. Its surface is covered in water, which is always moving. This includes massive oceans that shift with the tide and rivers that carve canyons by gently eroding the land over millions of years, not to forget the icy poles that cover vast swathes of the north and south. All this water is also constantly evaporating into the sky to form clouds, before coming back down as rain and snow.

Beneath the waves and deep underground, tectonic plates are slowly rumbling along as well. Driven by the heat of a molten heart at the Earth's core, these shifting plates have slowly shaped all of the planet's continents and will eventually tear them apart. They've also caused earthquakes and volcanic eruptions, as well as helping to create looming mountain ranges and sunken marine trenches. All of this makes our planet an amazing place to explore. So read on to discover how our planet works, the many biomes and ecosystems it supports and how we've learnt to make sense of it all.

WORD SEARCH

```
T H S Z B Y V B W J P A S I A
Q A O W Y E A A Q Z X F A W E
S F U J N T M Z J Z Q O I K I
F R T C K L U U B E N I G X W
Z I H W H E S F H H B R M B H
Z C A P W V W C G K K A J L K
R A M Q L V E W B G V O D P H
V M E N O R T H A M E R I C A
S Y R Z O Z K J L F M N I C V
I X I X Y E Y G E U R O P E C
X O C B N N G I O T O D C J T
C A A Q I I J T W G Y N Y Q A
X N H I L D E Y W C P D Z C E
U A N T A R C T I C A I P J M
C J P M F S A U S T R A L I A
```

AFRICA   ASIA   NORTH AMERICA

ANTARCTICA   SOUTH AMERICA

EUROPE   AUSTRALIA

DID YOU KNOW?

Scientists think Earth is around 4.54 billion years old.

SPOT THE DIFFERENCE

Can you find all five differences between these pictures of Earth?

ICE GIANTS

Mostly formed during the last ice age, glaciers are huge sheets of squashed snow that slowly move as they melt.

THE GREAT LAKES

Despite its name, the world's largest lake is the Caspian Sea. This is because it's completely surrounded by land.

A CHANGING LANDSCAPE

The world is full of physical structures like naturally formed hills and valleys, but also increasingly man-made roads and cities.

THE DRIEST PLACE ON EARTH

A desert is anywhere that gets less than 25ml of rain a year. It can be hot and sandy, but also ice-cold or even coastal.

BLUE PLANET

Though we call it 'Earth', 70 per cent of its surface is made up of oceans, most of which we haven't explored.

ISLANDS IN THE STREAM

One in six people live on an island, which describes anywhere that's surrounded by water, but is smaller than a continent.

GO WITH THE FLOW

Rivers crisscross the planet flowing from hills and mountains to the sea. The world's longest is the Nile in Africa.

LIFE IS EVERYWHERE

There are 8.7 million species of plants and animals, all of which depend on each other and the physical world to survive.

REACH FOR THE SKIES

Spiky outcrops of earth and rock, every mountain is at least 600 metres high. Otherwise, we call them hills.

WATCH THIS! SEE A LION!

SCAN WITH YOUR PHONE OR TABLET

https://bit.ly/3p32IXs

© Getty

BIOMES

Have you noticed that there are deserts all over the world? Even though they're in three different continents, the Sahara in North Africa, the Mojave in the United States and the Arabian desert in the Middle East have a lot in common. They all share a blazing hot climate and dusty landscape, which has forced plants and animals to adapt to survive, whether that's American cacti that store water in their spiky stems or camels that carry it in their humps.

This is what we call a 'biome': a large area with similar landscapes, weather and wildlife. Beyond deserts, our planet's other major land biomes include woodlands, grasslands and tundras. Some of these can be sorted into even smaller groups, such as temperate, tropical and taiga forests.

There are also biomes beneath the waves. Marine biomes include the ocean, coral reefs and estuaries, while freshwater biomes include ponds, rivers and lakes. All are surrounded by land and contain little to no salt.

While a biome can be made up of lots of ecosystems, all the plants and animals that live in it developed traits to help them thrive there. Just as cacti and camels have adapted to the heat, polar bears are built for the cold. They have evolved white coats to help them blend into the Arctic's snow-covered tundra. They would struggle to sneak up on their prey and catch food in any other biome, or if their native environment's climate changes.

This shows why it's important that we preserve biomes to protect plants and animals. We can do this by using fewer fossil fuels that cause global warming, as well as being careful about not cutting down too many trees, growing crops and overfishing.

TEMPERATE FOREST

TEMPERATURE: Wet and mild

With a gentle climate and four distinct seasons, deers, squirrels and hawks live here, while most trees drop their leaves in winter.

TROPICAL RAINFOREST

TEMPERATURE: Hot and humid

Found near the equator, this jungle biome is home to tall trees and rich, varied wildlife, such as monkeys, parrots and anacondas.

SAVANNAH

TEMPERATURE: Hot and dry

Only grasses and shrubs grow here, but it's home to lots of animals, such as elephants, zebras and lions.

DID YOU KNOW?

A third of the world is covered by forest biomes in all their many forms.

TAIGA FOREST

TEMPERATURE: Dry and cold

Found just south of the tundra with long winters. Moose, wolves and beavers live among hardy evergreen trees.

TUNDRA

TEMPERATURE: Wet and cold

Home to long, dark winters. Wild yaks and snow leopards live here, while plants are limited to lichens and mosses.

GRASSLANDS

TEMPERATURE: Dry and mild

Large herbivores like bison and wild horses graze on grasses and wildflowers in wide open plains alongside eagles, bobcats and weasels.

DESERTS

TEMPERATURE: Dry

While not all deserts are hot, they are all rainless, making them a hard place for plants and animals to live.

BIOME BAFFLER

Can you unscramble these words to spell the names of three biomes?

AGAIT   **ARISEN FORT**   **DAGSSNARLS**

....

© Getty

ECOSYSTEMS

A forest is like a football team. It sounds odd, but it's true. From the goalkeeper and attack to midfield and defence, a team is made up of lots of different roles. Each player does an important job, but they can't win on their own, so they work together. The same is true of all plants, animals and microorganisms in woodland. But rather than wanting to share a league trophy, these creatures depend on each other and their habitat to live. We call this an ecosystem.

There are three jobs in an ecosystem: producer, consumer and decomposer. The trees in the forest produce their own food, turning sunshine into chemical energy through a process called photosynthesis. Deers can't make their own food, so they consume – or eat – the trees' leaves. However, deers don't just eat; sometimes *they* get eaten by hungry wolves.

Finally, insects, mushrooms and bacteria will feed on dead plants, deers' uneaten bones and even the wolves' poo! These tiny creatures decompose – or break down – the remains into molecules like water, carbon and nitrogen. These molecules become part of the soil and air, which helps plants grow so the ecosystem can keep on going.

Beyond the forest, ecosystems come in lots of shapes and sizes. A back garden or even a giant ocean can be an ecosystem. The key thing is that an ecosystem has to be balanced. You might think it's cruel that predators eat prey, but if there weren't enough wolves to eat deers, deers would eat too many leaves. This wouldn't be good for the trees, which need leaves to photosynthesise, and this would mean the deers would eventually struggle to find food. Changes to climate and natural disasters can unbalance ecosystems. People can also upset them by polluting and clearing land for building and farming.

FILL IN THE FOOD CHAIN

Can you work out the names of all the creatures in this ecosystem from the missing letters?

H...WK

SN...KE

R....BB....T

G....AS....

WATCH THIS!
WHAT IS AN ECOSYSTEM?

SCAN WITH YOUR PHONE OR TABLET

https://bit.ly/3zHM84u

PRODUCER, CONSUMER, DECOMPOSER

Sort the plants and animals by the role they play

HUMAN

CARROT

SNAIL

COW

CROCODILE

APPLE TREE

MUSHROOM

ELEPHANT

SEAWEED

SUNFLOWER

BACTERIA

WORM

PRODUCERS

....

....

....

....

....

....

CONSUMER

....

....

....

....

....

....

DECOMPOSER

....

....

....

....

....

....

Answers: 1. APPLE TREE, 2. SEAWEED, 3. SUNFLOWER, 4. CARROT

Answers: 1. HUMAN, 2. CROCODILE, 3. COW, 4. ELEPHANT

Answers: 1. SNAIL, 2. WORM, 3. MUSHROOM, 4. BACTERIA

TOPOGRAPHY

Imagine you're going on a journey. It might be to the next town over or a far-off country. Either way, you might use a map to plan how you're going to get there. But to do that, you need to know how to read one.

This starts with knowing what time of map you're using. A political map will show you the boundaries of countries, counties and cities, while a topographic map shows the shape of the planet's surface, such as landforms – natural features like lakes and valleys. Most maps will include a mix of political and topographic features to help you navigate.

But you still might struggle to recognise what you're looking at. In the past, mapmakers used to draw landmarks like mountains and castles. This artwork was often very pretty and easy to understand, but it meant maps were cluttered and not very detailed. Today's maps use simple symbols to represent things instead. For instance, the letter P on a map means there is a car park there.

Your map might also have squiggly lines called contours. These tell you the elevation of the land – that's how high or low it is. When the lines are far apart, it means the land is gently sloped. But when they're closer together, the land will be steep, forming a hill or a mountain. This is really helpful to know if you're planning to hike somewhere.

Anywhere in the world can be located using a system called longitude and latitude. They often look like a grid when printed on a map. Lines of latitude run east and west, while lines of longitude run north and south. Each one has its own number, which are known as degrees. Together, you can use these two numbers as coordinates to find where you're going – or tell someone else – without knowing the address.

SYMBOLS

These show where you can find landmarks and other places. A key shows you what all the symbols mean.

LINES OF LONGITUDE

You can measure how east or west somewhere is with these lines, which start at the Prime Meridian in Greenwich, UK.

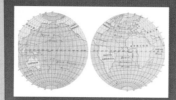

CONTOUR LINES

These lines show high and low areas of land. The closer together they are, the steeper it is.

PLACE NAMES

Some maps include the names of towns, cities, roads and rivers to help you find your way.

MAP QUIZ

Can you guess what each of the map symbols mean?

1.

A) Campsite ☐
B) Museum ☐
C) Castle ☐

3.

A) Railway line ☐
B) Motorway ☐
C) Footpath ☐

2.

A) Petrol station ☐
B) Car park ☐
C) Post office ☐

4.

A) Site of a battle ☐
B) Place with a view ☐
C) Place of worship ☐

ANSWERS: 1. CAMPSITE, 2. CAR PARK, 3. FOOTPATH, 4. PLACE WITH A VIEW

LINES OF LATITUDE

You can see how north or south somewhere is using these imaginary lines, which run parallel to the Equator.

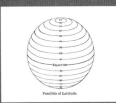

SHOWING DIRECTION

Maps are usually printed with north at the top, but you can double check by seeing what way the compass rose points.

SENSE OF SCALE

The scale shows how distances on a map relate to the actual distances, so 1:50,000 would mean 1cm on the map, which equals 50,000cm (500m) in the real world.

LANDFORMS

Maps show the naturally formed shapes that make up Earth's surface, like mountains, forests and rivers.

DID YOU KNOW?

The world's oldest map, the Imago Mundi, was created by ancient Babylonians over 2,622 years ago.

GLACIERS

A glacier is like a flowing river of ice. It's a thick, frozen mound that moves under its weight, if only very slowly – usually around one metre a day. But even at this plodding pace, glaciers have the power to transform landscapes.

Most glaciers are at the North and South Poles, although you can also find them high in mountain ranges. The world's largest is the Lambert Glacier in Antarctica, which is 400km long and 250km wide. That's only a bit smaller than Iceland or Kentucky.

Glaciers emerge when snow doesn't melt, so it piles up and turns into solid ice. This can take a very long time. Some of the youngest glaciers are around 200 years old, while many more are left over from the Ice Age that ended 10,000 years ago. As they slowly slide downhill, glaciers scrape and grind the surrounding rock. Acting like a pencil sharpener, a glacier can give a mountain a pointed peak, like the Matterhorn in the Alps. They can also flatten the floor of valleys, which is how the fjords in Norway and Chile were created. Glaciers can pick up giant boulders and carry them far away, leaving them mysteriously out of place in flat lowlands like the Okotoks Erratic in Canada.

Glaciers also store more than half the fresh water on the planet. As mountain glaciers reach the foothill where it's warmer, the ice can feed lakes and rivers, while parts of polar glaciers will break off – or 'calve' – along coastlines to form icebergs.

But as the world's temperature heats up, glaciers are shrinking. This has led to some incredible discoveries in the retreating ice, uncovering lost Viking treasure in Norway and a perfectly preserved mammoth in Siberia. But it also means more meltwater is running into the oceans, adding to the rising sea levels.

TRUE OR FALSE?

PAKISTAN HAS MORE ICEBERGS THAN ANYWHERE ON EARTH, EXCEPT THE POLES.

TRUE ☐ OR FALSE ☐

Answer: True - it has 7,253

POP QUIZ

WHICH OF THESE CONTINENTS DOESN'T HAVE ANY GLACIERS?

☐ AFRICA

☐ ANTARCTICA

☐ AUSTRALIA

Answer: Australia

END OF THE LINE

Near the end – or snout – of the glacier, the snow melts in the summer months, leaving behind rocks known as moraine.

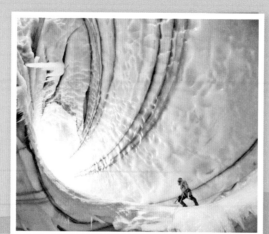

ICE, ICE BABY

As more and more snow piles up, the weight builds and squeezes the bottom layers so hard that it turns to ice.

CRACKS START TO SHOW

Because of friction, the top of a glacier moves faster than the bottom, which can lead to huge cracks on the surface.

LET IT SNOW

A glacier starts in the highland areas of mountains, where the snow falls but doesn't melt because it's too cold.

GO WITH THE FLOW

Under its own weight, the ice slowly slips down the mountainside, taking rocks and dirt – known as moraine – with it.

WATCH THIS!

ALL ABOUT GLACIERS

SCAN WITH YOUR PHONE OR TABLET

https://bit.ly/3SEwxeo

© Getty

OCEANS

Earth is a lot wetter than you may realise. The oceans cover three quarters of the planet's surface. While this is one massive body of salt water, we divide it into five regions: the Atlantic, Pacific, Indian, Arctic and Southern.

Water is constantly moving around the oceans in patterns called currents. As these currents flow, they move cold and warm water from one place to another. This changes the weather and climate on land. For instance, the UK would be as cold as Canada if it wasn't warmed by the Gulf Stream travelling from the Caribbean, while Peru is chillier than most tropical countries because the Humboldt Current carries water from icy Antarctica along its coastline.

Ocean currents also help move anything that floats in them, acting like a fast lane for ships and sea life. Jellyfish, sea turtles and sharks all use the currents to move quickly between feeding and breeding grounds. Smaller fish also latch onto larger animals to hitch a ride.

As well as covering the whole world, the oceans are incredibly deep. Almost 11,000m beneath the waves, the Marina Trench in the Pacific Ocean is the deepest place in the world. If you could drop Mount Everest down there, the peak wouldn't reach the water's surface. Only three people have ever been to the bottom of the trench.

The size of the oceans mean they're home to more types of animals than anywhere else. While fish have gills that allow them to breathe underwater, dolphins, seals and whales need to go to the surface to inhale air. Some have no limbs, such as clams and sea urchins, while others have many, like octopus and giant squid. As the deep ocean gets no sunlight, many sea creatures glow in the dark, like the angler fish.

DID YOU KNOW?

We've explored more of Mars than we have the ocean floor.

PACIFIC

HOW YOU PRONOUNCE MY NAME

PAH-SI-FIHK

SURFACE AREA: 165 million km²
AVERAGE DEPTH: 4,280M

Covering one third of the world's surface, the Pacific is both the largest and deepest ocean. It separates Asia and Australia from North and South America.

SOUTHERN

HOW YOU PRONOUNCE MY NAME

SUTH-URN

SURFACE AREA: 20 million km²
AVERAGE DEPTH: 3,270M

Sitting at the South Pole, this is the 'youngest' ocean. It only emerged 30 million years ago when South America and Antarctica moved apart.

ATLANTIC

HOW YOU PRONOUNCE MY NAME

UHT-LAN-TUHK

SURFACE AREA: 106 million km²
AVERAGE DEPTH: 4,280M

The second largest ocean divides what European explorers called the 'Old World' of Europe and Africa from the 'New World' of North and South America.

OCEAN PROMOTION

Label this map with the names of the oceans.

1 ....

2 ....

4 ....

3 ....

5 ....

INDIAN

 HOW YOU PRONOUNCE MY NAME IN-DEE–UN

SURFACE AREA: 70.5 million km²
AVERAGE DEPTH: 3,741M

Located between Asia, Africa and Australia, the Indian is the world's warmest ocean. It's also the largest breeding ground for humpback whales.

ARCTIC

 HOW YOU PRONOUNCE MY NAME AAK-TUHK

SURFACE AREA: 14 million km²
AVERAGE DEPTH: 987M

The smallest and shallowest ocean, the Arctic is the area around the North Pole. It's covered in ice for most of the year.

RIVERS

A river is a ribbon of fresh, flowing water. You can find them crisscrossing the land on every continent. Rivers come in all shapes and sizes, though smaller ones are sometimes called brooks or streams.

The starting point of any river is known as the source. The water can come from rain, melting snow or bubbles up from underground springs. Rivers always move downhill due to gravity. The water runs straight and fast down steep mountaintops, creating rapids and waterfalls. Rivers then widen and slow down as they reach flatlands. The end of a river is called a mouth. This is where the water empties into the ocean, a lake or even another river. A stream that feeds into a bigger one is called a tributary.

Rivers carve a path – or 'channel' – as they move across the land. They bend when they reach objects such as hills or large rocks that are too big for them to move. But over a long period of time, rivers wear down their surroundings, becoming broader and deeper. This can reshape the landscape. The mighty Colorado River in the United States made the Grand Canyon, while the Zambezi has cut a great gorge beneath Victoria Falls in Zimbabwe.

The stone, sand and soil rivers wash away are carried downstream. Over the years, this material builds up to form a delta, which carves the river into smaller, shallower branches. It's also full of rich, wet soil that's great for farming. This spills over onto the land whenever the river floods.

It's perhaps no surprise that rivers are home to all sorts of wildlife. This includes many insects, as well as freshwater fish like salmon, trout, carp and catfish. Depending on where you are in the world, you will also find ducks, kingfishers, otters, beavers, snakes, salamanders and crocodiles.

AMAZON RIVER

HOW YOU PRONOUNCE MY NAME A-MUH-ZUHN RI-VUH

LOCATION: South America
LENGTH: 6,500km
MAX WIDTH: 100km
MAX DEPTH: 100m

Fed by 1,100 tributaries, this mighty river carries one-fifth of the world's freshwater as it curls through South America's giant rainforest.

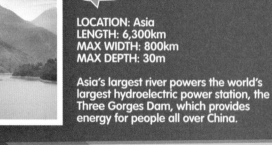

YANGTZE

HOW YOU PRONOUNCE MY NAME YANGKT-SEE

LOCATION: Asia
LENGTH: 6,300km
MAX WIDTH: 800km
MAX DEPTH: 30m

Asia's largest river powers the world's largest hydroelectric power station, the Three Gorges Dam, which provides energy for people all over China.

MISSISSIPPI RIVER

 HOW YOU PRONOUNCE MY NAME MI-SUH-SI-PEE RI-VUH

LOCATION: North America
LENGTH: 3,770km
MAX WIDTH: 18km
MAX DEPTH: 61m

Nicknamed 'Old Man River', the Mississippi travels through the heart of the United States and is a highway for trade, carrying 12,000 ships a year.

RIVER RIDDLER

Rearrange the letters to spell the name of six features of a river

1 **CRUSOE** → ....
2 **HOTMU** → ....
3 **BKAN** → ....
4 **LNHCNAE** → ....
5 **TDELA** → ....
6 **ARTYBRUIT** → ....

DID YOU KNOW?

Caño Cristales in Colombia is called the 'River of Five Colours', as its waters turn blue, red, black, yellow and green as it moves downstream.

DANUBE

 **HOW YOU PRONOUNCE MY NAME** DAN-YOOB

LOCATION: Europe
LENGTH: 2,850km
MAX WIDTH: 1.5km
MAX DEPTH: 178m

Stretching from Germany's Black Forest to the Black Sea, the Danube passes through 10 countries and four capital cities: Vienna, Bratislava, Budapest (pictured) and Belgrade.

GANGES

 HOW YOU PRONOUNCE MY NAME GAN-JEEZ

LOCATION: Asia
LENGTH: 2525km
MAX WIDTH: 11km
MAX DEPTH: 33m

Flowing through India and Bangladesh, the Ganges is sacred to millions of Hindus, who believe the river's water purifies the soul and heals the body.

NILE

 HOW YOU PRONOUNCE MY NAME NILE

LOCATION: Africa
LENGTH: 6,650km
MAX WIDTH: 2.8km
MAX DEPTH: 11m

The world's longest river flows through eastern Africa, where its waters and the rich soil of its delta have been essential to farming for thousands of years.

ISLANDS OF THE WORLD

Picture yourself on an island. Is it a spit of sand with only a palm tree sticking out of it? Can you hear the sound of crashing waves as you lie in the tropical sunshine? In reality, you're just as likely to be in a crowded city as a lone castaway. You could be miles inland on a river or lake rather than far out at sea, and it might be too wet or cold for sunbathing. That's because an island is any area of land that's surrounded by water, but there are also two main types.

Continental islands are close to other land masses. Some, like Madagascar and Greenland, were made when continents were torn apart by shifting tectonic plates. Others, like Great Britain were formed by monstrous floods, which covered low-lying land and only left the tops of hills above the water level.

Oceanic islands are found far out at sea. They are created by underwater volcanoes that build up layers of lava over millions of years until they break the water's surface. Iceland, the Philippines and Japan were all created this way.

Sometimes a coral reef will grow over a sunken volcanic island. As the reef rises above the water it will become an atoll. This type of island is normally ring-shaped with a lagoon in the middle. However they're formed, a group of islands is known as an archipelago. Indonesia is the biggest archipelago in the world, with 17,508 islands, of which about 6,000 are inhabited. Islands can be home to some weird and wonderful wildlife. Cut off from the wider world, creatures often evolve very differently from their mainland cousins. Some grow really big, like the komodo dragon and giant tortoise, while others shrink, such as the Seychelles frog, which is the size of an ant!

GREENLAND

 HOW YOU PRONOUNCE MY NAME — GREEN-LUHND

LOCATION: Arctic
AREA: 2.1 million km²
POPULATION: 56,081

A third of the size of Australia and covered in ice all year round, Greenland is both the world's largest island and the least densely populated.

MADAGASCAR

 HOW YOU PRONOUNCE MY NAME — MA-DUH-GA-SKUH

LOCATION: Africa
AREA: 587,040 km²
POPULATION: 28 million

Around 80 per cent of the plants and animals on this island off the eastern coast of Africa can be found nowhere else in the world.

GREAT BRITAIN

 HOW YOU PRONOUNCE MY NAME — GRAYT BRI-TN

LOCATION: Europe
AREA: 209,331 km²
POPULATION: 61 million

Europe's biggest island was joined to the continent until a giant tsunami 9,000 years ago drowned the lowlands in between.

HONSHU

HOW YOU PRONOUNCE MY NAME HON-SHOO

LOCATION: Asia
AREA: 227,960 km²
POPULATION: 104 million

The largest island that makes up the country of Japan, it is home to both the capital city of Tokyo and the iconic Mount Fuji.

HAWAII

HOW YOU PRONOUNCE MY NAME HUH-WY-EE

LOCATION: Pacific
AREA: 28,311 km²
POPULATION: 1.4 million

More than 6,000km from the rest of the United States, Hawaii is an archipelago that continues to grow as the volcanoes Mauna Loa and Kilauea regularly spill lava into the sea.

MALDIVES

HOW YOU PRONOUNCE MY NAME MOL-DEEVZ

LOCATION: Asia
AREA: 300 km²
POPULATION: 540,542

As rising sea levels are slowly drowning this chain of coral islands, Maldivian leaders are considering evacuating everyone that lives there to Sri Lanka or India.

ISLE SPY

Can you work out the names of these types of islands from the missing letters?

1 ....TOL

2 ....RCH....P....L....G....

3 C....NT....N....NT....L

4 ....CEAN....C

WATCH THIS!
TOUR THE MALDIVES

SCAN WITH YOUR PHONE OR TABLET
https://bit.ly/3Pa1UdW

MOUNTAIN RANGES

You can't miss a mountain range. These mighty mounds of rock rise out of the ground all over the world. People risk their lives to climb them. They form the boundaries of countries and continents, and even warp the weather around them.

The highest mountain ranges, like the Himalayas in Asia and Andes in South America, were created by shifting tectonic plates. Over millions of years, these massive slabs in Earth's crust crashed into one another, making the land above buckle and bend into mountains and valleys.

Other mountains started off as volcanoes. This happens when tectonic plates move in a way that sends molten rock spurting to the surface. This slowly builds up with each eruption to form one or more mountains.

Some volcanoes eventually stop spewing lava and become like other mountains, like Ben Nevis in Scotland. But many remain active, with around 25 erupting each year.

The bottom – or base – of a mountain range is often home to lush forests, fed by water that runs down from glaciers, lakes and melted snow. But for every 100 metres you climb, the temperature drops by one degree Celsius. Eventually, you reach the tree line, where it's too cold and windy for anything other than short plants like moose and lichen to grow.

But even these can't cope at the top of super-high mountains – all you'll find are snow-covered rocks! To survive, animals have to be hardy. Red pandas in the Himalayas grow an extra thick coat. Mountain goats and ibexes in Europe's Alps have tough but flexible hooves to balance on the uneven, rocky ground, while the Andean condor has an extra long wingspan so it can fly up 300km in a day to find food.

HIMALAYAS

HOW YOU PRONOUNCE MY NAME — HI-MUH-LAY-UHZ

LOCATION: Asia
HEIGHT: 8,850m
LENGTH: 2,400km

Skirting the border of northeast India, this mountain range is home to 30 of the world's tallest mountains, including Mount Everest and K2.

TOP OF THE PEAKS

Rank the tallest mountain on every continent in order of their size from tallest (1) to shortest (7)

MOUNT KOSCIUSZKO, AUSTRALIA

VINSON MASSIF, ANTARCTICA

KILIMANJARO, AFRICA

MOUNT EVEREST, ASIA

DENALI, NORTH AMERICA

ELBRUS, EUROPE

MOUNT ACONCAGUA, SOUTH AMERICA

1 - TALLEST
....

2
....

3
....

4
....

5
....

6
....

7 - SHORTEST
....

DID YOU KNOW?

The world's longest mountain range is almost entirely underwater and stretches for 6,500km.

ALPS

HOW YOU PRONOUNCE MY NAME — ALPS

LOCATION: Europe
HEIGHT: 4,809m
LENGTH: 1,200km

Mount Blanc is the highest peak in Europe's most extensive mountain range, which arcs across the continent from France to Slovenia.

ANDES

HOW YOU PRONOUNCE MY NAME — AN-DEEZ

LOCATION: South America
HEIGHT: 6,961m
LENGTH: 8,900km

The world's longest mountain range (at least above ground) runs all the way down South America, but is very narrow, rarely more than 320km wide.

ATLAS MOUNTAINS

HOW YOU PRONOUNCE MY NAME — GREEN-LUHND

LOCATION: Africa
HEIGHT: 4,167m
LENGTH: 2,500km

Forming the backbone of Morocco, Algeria and Tunisia, this mountain range is broken up with areas of high, flat land known as plateaus.

ROCKY MOUNTAINS

HOW YOU PRONOUNCE MY NAME — ROK-KEE MOWN-TNZ

LOCATION: North America
HEIGHT: 4,400m
LENGTH: 4,828km

Made up of 100 different ranges, the 'Rockies' stretch from icy Alberta in Canada to the deserts of New Mexico in the USA.

URALS

HOW YOU PRONOUNCE MY NAME — YUOR-RUHLZ

LOCATION: Europe
HEIGHT: 1,895m
LENGTH: 2,500km

One of the world's oldest mountain ranges, the Urals stretch from the frozen Arctic coastline in Russia to Kazakhstan, dividing Europe and Asia.

LAKES

A lake is a body of water that's surrounded by land. There are millions of them worldwide. They can be found in every environment – wide open plains, up mountains and even in deserts.

Some lakes could fit in a back garden. Others are so big they're called seas. The Caspian Sea, which borders Europe and Asia, is the world's largest lake, with an area of more than 370,000km². That's almost as big as Japan! But while the northern Caspian is so shallow you can wade across it, Lake Baikal in Russia is so deep that it holds almost as much water as all four of the Great Lakes of North America put together.

There are lots of ways to make a lake. Many in the northern hemisphere were made over 18,000 years ago by ice sheets. These giant glaciers carved out bowl-shaped basins as they slowly moved across the land. Then when they melted, the water settled in these pits.

Tectonic plates deep inside Earth can also crack the planet's surface when they move. This can then fill with rain, stream water or melting snow to form a lake. When a volcano blows its top during an eruption, it can also form a crater that fills to become a lake.

If a lake is connected to a river, it's described as open and will have fresh water. If water only leaves a lake by evaporating, the lake is called closed and will contain salt water. That's because the mineral is often left behind when water vaporises.

As lakes come in so many different shapes, sizes and places, they can contain all sorts of wildlife. Freshwater lakes are home to everything from fish, frogs and swans to alligators and snakes, while crocodiles, crabs, and flamingos can be found in saltwater lakes.

LAKE TITICACA

HOW YOU PRONOUNCE MY NAME TI-TEE-KAA-KAA

LOCATION: South America
AREA: 8,372 km²
AVERAGE DEPTH: 107m

Despite being high in the Andes mountains, 3,800 metres above sea level, large boats still cross this lake to deliver goods between Bolivia and Peru.

LAKE TANGANYIKA

HOW YOU PRONOUNCE MY NAME TANG-GUH-NYEE-KUH

LOCATION: Africa
AREA: 2,900 km²
AVERAGE DEPTH: 570m

The longest lake in the world stretches for 673km and is shared between four African countries: Tanzania, Zambia, Democratic Republic of Congo and Burundi.

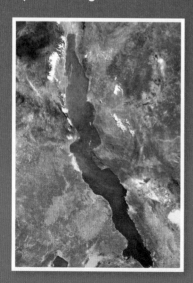

CUCKMERE HAVEN

HOW YOU PRONOUNCE MY NAME KUK-MEEUH HAY-VN

LOCATION: United Kingdom, Europe
AVERAGE DEPTH: 3m

This U-shaped pool, also known as an 'oxbow' lake, started out as a curve in a river until it was left behind when floodwaters cut a more direct path.

WORD SEARCH

Can you find the names of eight lakes from around the world?

```
C O M O O X H R T L
C N T G S J B S Q L
J A U M U C A T B O
Q B Z E P W I A M C
Z T T V E E K H Z H
U Q U O R W A O K N
S A F S I L L E J E
V I C T O R I A W S
R B E O R E W V I S
X I F K Z A T P S C
```

VICTORIA · **XI** · **VOSTOK**

LOCH NESS · **SUPERIOR**

TAHOE · **COMO** · **BAIKAL**

DEAD SEA

HOW YOU PRONOUNCE MY NAME DED SEE

LOCATION: Middle East
AREA: 605 km²
AVERAGE DEPTH: 199m

This lake bordering Israel and Jordan gets its spooky name because it's ten times saltier than sea water and no fish or seaweed can survive in it.

LAKE MEAD

HOW YOU PRONOUNCE MY NAME MEED

LOCATION: United States, North America
AREA: 640 km²
AVERAGE DEPTH: 162m

This artificial lake was created when the Hoover Dam was built in 1931. It stops the Colorado River flooding as well as providing water and generating electricity for nearby people.

LAKE BAIKAL

HOW YOU PRONOUNCE MY NAME BAI-KAAL

LOCATION: Russia
AREA: 31,722 km²
AVERAGE DEPTH: 744m

You'd have to swim the equivalent of 40 lengths of an Olympic swimming pool to reach the bottom of the world's deepest lake.

DID YOU KNOW?

There are over 187,000 lakes in Finland.

DESERTS

There's nowhere more extreme than a desert. They can be burning hot or freezing cold, but they're always very dry, getting less than 250mm of rain a year.

They can be rocky as well as sandy, as there are few plants to protect the soil from the wind, so it's blown away, revealing the surface beneath. Rare flash floods also create steep scarps and gullies.

You can find deserts all over the world and on every continent. But most can be found near 30 degrees latitude north and south of the equator. This is because hot air rises in the tropics and then settles in this region, baking the land and evaporating any water.

Deserts are also often found on the western edges of continents. This is because cold ocean currents affect any moist air that passes over it, making it rain at sea before it reaches the land.

Mountain ranges can have a similar effect. Air cools as it passes over the peaks, so it rains or snows there rather than in the land below. The Gobi may have dried out in the so-called 'rain shadow' of the Himalayas.

While they can be challenging places to live, deserts are far from barren wastelands. We have already talked about how camels and cacti have adapted to store water. Many other creatures have found alternative ways to live here too. For example, Gila monsters burrow underground to escape the heat, while the fennec fox only comes out at night when it's cool, and hawks and eagles crisscross the skies, flying much further to find food.

One in every six people live in a desert. Inventions like irrigation, cars and air conditioning make it easier to live in these extreme conditions today. But human activities, such as farming too many animals in one place or cutting down lots of trees, are also causing new deserts to form.

DID YOU KNOW?

Only one in five deserts are sandy.

ATACAMA

 HOW YOU PRONOUNCE MY NAME — A-TUH-KAA-MUH

LOCATION: Chile, South America
AREA: 104,741 km²
AVERAGE TEMPERATURE: 18°C
AVERAGE YEARLY RAINFALL: 15mm

The world's driest non-polar desert, parts of it get less than a millimetre of rain a year. It's so harsh that astronauts use it to prepare for exploring Mars.

SAHARA

 HOW YOU PRONOUNCE MY NAME — SUH-HAA-RUH

LOCATION: North Africa
AREA: 9.2 million km²
AVERAGE TEMPERATURE: 20°C
AVERAGE YEARLY RAINFALL: 76mm

Covering northern Africa, the world's largest hot desert can reach a blistering 50°C during the summer, while its sand dunes can be up to 180 metres high.

ANTARCTICA

 HOW YOU PRONOUNCE MY NAME — AN-TAAK-TUH-HAH

LOCATION: South Pole
AREA: 14.2 million km²
AVERAGE TEMPERATURE: -49°C
AVERAGE YEARLY RAINFALL: 166mm

The little precipitation this frozen continent gets is mainly snow. Unlike hot deserts, where water evaporates, this snow just piles up year after year.

GOBI

 HOW YOU PRONOUNCE MY NAME — GOW-BEE

LOCATION: Central Asia
AREA: 1,295,000 km²
AVERAGE TEMPERATURE: -2.5°C
AVERAGE YEARLY RAINFALL: 194mm

Covering large parts of Mongolia and China, this cold, rocky desert is a treasure trove for fossil hunters, with a fifth of known dinosaurs discovered here.

CHIHUAHUAN

HOW YOU PRONOUNCE MY NAME CHUH-WAA-WAAN

LOCATION: North America
AREA: 501,896 km²
AVERAGE TEMPERATURE: 18˚C
AVERAGE YEARLY RAINFALL: 235mm

Stretching from the southwestern United States and deep into Mexico, North America's largest desert is also the world's most biologically diverse, with over 500 cactus species.

GREAT VICTORIA

HOW YOU PRONOUNCE MY NAME GRAYT VUHK-TAW-REE-UH

LOCATION: Australia
AREA: 422,466 km²
AVERAGE TEMPERATURE: 32˚C
AVERAGE YEARLY RAINFALL: 200mm

Many Aboriginal people have lived in Australia's largest desert, which is made up of red sand dunes and arid grasslands, for more than 24,000 years.

DESERT DECODER

Can you unscramble these words to spell the names of three deserts?

AM JOVE

....

AILA HARK

....

ACTIVATOR GERI

....

FIND THE MATCHING CACTUS!

Can you find the two matching cacti in this Mexican desert?

END OF THE CHAPTER: OUR PLANET

S o now you have the lay of the land – and the sea. The planet is a varied place, with arid deserts and deep oceans, frozen glaciers and explosive volcanoes. These physical features are shaped by never-ending natural processes. This includes the push and pull of tectonic plates in the bowels of Earth, making mountain ranges and islands. But the rain, rivers and ocean waves also play an important role, carving the lumps and bumps of terrain that appear as contour lines on a map.

Where places are in the world also affects what they look like. The poles are icy because they get very little sunshine, while the equator is hot because it gets more sun than anywhere else. These hot and cold zones also affect which way the wind blows and where it rains, shaping the climates of temperate and tropical zones.

Areas with similar landscapes, climates and wildlife are known as biomes. This includes the tundra, savannah, tropical rainforests and more. Plants and animals adapt to live in these particular environments. They also form ecosystems that rely on each other – as well as the land itself – to survive. So it's important we protect them by thinking about what impact we have on the world, from making sure we don't pollute places to combating climate change.

WHAT HAVE YOU LEARNED?

Fill in the blanks with the supplied words to complete the ten sentences.

1 THE PLANET'S SURFACE IS COVERED IN... .... LIKE HILLS, MOUNTAINS AND VALLEYS.

2 LINES OF... ....RUN EAST AND WEST, WHILE LINES OF... ....RUN NORTH AND SOUTH.

3 THERE ARE THREE ROLES PLANTS AND ANIMALS PLAY IN EVERY ECOSYSTEM: ...., ...CONSUMER AND DECOMPOSER.

4 PLANTS AND ANIMALS DEVELOP SPECIAL TRAITS TO... ....TO DIFFERENT BIOMES.

5 WHILE YOU FIND BIG ANIMALS LIKE LIONS AND ELEPHANTS ON THE... ...., ...ONLY GRASS AND SHRUBS GROW HERE.

6 MOUNT ....IN THE... ....IS THE WORLD'S TALLEST MOUNTAIN.

7 A DESERT CAN BE EITHER HOT OR COLD, BUT IT'S ALWAYS VERY... ....AND GETS LITTLE RAIN.

8 WHILE A MOUNTAIN... ....CAN FEED INTO LAKES, NEAR THE OCEAN THE ICE CAN BREAK OFF AND BECOME AN... ....

9 THE START OF A RIVER IS CALLED THE... ....WHILE THE END IS KNOWN AS THE... ....

10 THERE ARE... ....OCEANS, THE LARGEST IS CALLED THE... ....

DRY
SOURCE
SAVANNAH
FIVE
EVEREST
DISSOLVES
ICEBERG
MOUTH
LATITUDE
LANDFORMS
PRODUCER
PACIFIC
GLACIER
HIMALAYAS
LONGITUDE

ANSWERS: 1. Landforms, 2. Longitude, Latitude, 3. Producer, 4. Adapt, 5. Savannah, 6. Everest, Himalayas, 7. Dry, 8. Glacier, Iceberg, 9. Source, Mouth, 10. Five, Pacific

PLANET PUZZLES

TRUE OR FALSE?

Deserts can be hot or cold.

TRUE ☐ OR FALSE ☐

LAND HOY!

Can you find the right way to the island?

WHERE DO I BELONG?

Now you know all about biomes, join up the right plants and animals with where they live.

TIGER

TROPICAL RAINFOREST

SAVANNAH

DESERT

TUNDRA

MOOSE

WILDEBEEST

CACTUS

ANSWERS: TIGER / RAINFOREST, WILDEBEEST / SAVANNAH, MOOSE / TUNDRA / MOOSE, CACTUS / DESERT

SPOT THE DIFFERENCE

Find five differences between these two river scenes

ANSWERS

FIND THE LATITUDE AND LONGITUDE

Now you can know all about topography, can you give the coordinates for these places?

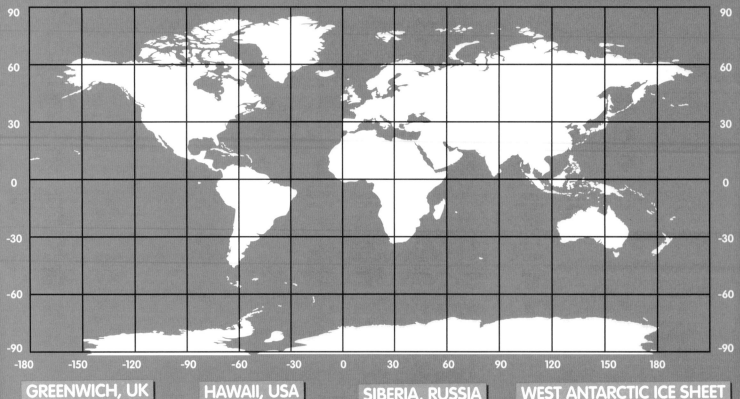

GREENWICH, UK

....

HAWAII, USA

....

SIBERIA, RUSSIA

....

WEST ANTARCTIC ICE SHEET

....

CAPE OF GOOD HOPE, SOUTH AFRICA

....

BORNEO, MALAYSIA

....

AMAZON, BRAZIL

....

TERRAIN BRAINTEASERS

Can you unscramble these words to spell out the names of the planet's main features?

EETRSD

....

CLIRAGE

....

SDLNIA

....

KLEA

....

ANSWERS (From top): Desert, Glacier, Island, Lake

DOWNHILL DOT-TO-DOT

Join the dots to reveal the picture of the mountain skier

DO YOU KNOW HOW TO NAVIGATE?

Label the four points of a compass.

 ....

 ....

TRUE OR FALSE?

Glaciers usually move 1 metre a day.

TRUE ☐ OR FALSE ☐

ANSWERS: True

33

THE WORLD

Looking down from space, you can learn a lot about Earth. An alien flying through our solar system could clearly see how big our oceans are and that the polar ice caps are frozen. They could work out that green swathes of land are forests, while golden brown patches are deserts. If they've got a really good eye – or perhaps several – they might even pick out the tallest mountain or longest river. But this picture only tells half the story.

Beyond the natural planet, there's the human world. From high above, our alien explorer would be able to see some signs of who we are, such as the physical towns and cities we live in, the farms that feed us or the roads that connect them. But they wouldn't be able to work out where one country begins and another ends. These border lines are rarely physical. Instead, they're agreed on by those who live there.

In this chapter, we're going to take a grand tour of all the continents and their major countries. We will explore their capital cities and famous landmarks, and learn about the customs, cultures and languages of the people that make these places unique.

LINGO BINGO

In Germany people talk in German, but in Peru they speak Spanish, so it's not always obvious what the official language of a country is. Join the correct language to the country it is spoken in.

PORTUGUESE
Greeting: "Olá"
Official language in 10 countries and territories

ENGLISH
Greeting: "Hello"
Official language in 10 countries and territories

ARABIC
Greeting: "Marhaba"
Official language in 10 countries and territories

MANDARIN
Greeting: "Ni hao"
Official language in 10 countries and territories

EGYPT

BRAZIL

CHINA

AUSTRALIA

ANSWERS: Portuguese - Brazil, English - Australia, Arabic - Egypt, Mandarin - China

FUN WITH FLAGS

Can you tell which country this banner belongs to?

1
A) India
B) Mexico
C) Ireland

2
A) Belgium
B) Italy
C) France

3
A) China
B) Vietnam
C) Cuba

ANSWERS: 1 - India, 2 - France, 3 - Vietnam

© Getty

35

There are 193 countries in the world.

NORTH AMERICA

HOW YOU PRONOUNCE MY NAME NAWTH UH-MEH-RUH-KUH

SIZE: 24.7 million km²
POPULATION: 592 million
NUMBER OF COUNTRIES: 23

Canada, the United States and Mexico dominate, but North America also includes many Central American countries and numerous island nations.

MAP OF THE WORLD

The world is made up of seven continents. Europe, North America and most of Asia are in the northern hemisphere. Australia, Antarctica and most of South America are in the southern hemisphere. Finally, there's Africa, which straddles both hemispheres.

Europe and Asia are joined together, with Russia spread across both of them. North and South America are connected by the narrow strip of Panama. The real difference between these continents is cultural. Each has its own identity, with people who speak similar languages, have political ties and share religions.

But this doesn't mean that continents are united. Instead, they are divided up into lots of countries. These can cover huge areas like Australia, China and Canada, or be very small like the island nation of Nauru or Vatican City, which covers less than a square kilometre. They are often also home to different groups of people, who may speak more than one language. But every country has a single government, which is led by a leader, such as a king or queen, president or prime minister.

Antarctica is a special case. The coldest and windiest place in the world, no one has successfully settled on the continent. Instead, many countries work together to protect Antarctica's wildlife.

SOUTH AMERICA

HOW YOU PRONOUNCE MY NAME SAWTH UH-MEH-RUH-KUH

SIZE: 17.8 million km²
POPULATION: 423 million
NUMBER OF COUNTRIES: 12

Home to countries that include Argentina, Bolivia, Brazil and Chile, three in every five people on this continent speak Spanish.

TRUE OR FALSE?

THERE USED TO BE ONLY ONE REALLY BIG CONTINENT.

TRUE ☐ OR FALSE ☐

ANSWER: True - it was called Pangea.

EUROPE

HOW YOU PRONOUNCE MY NAME YUOR-RUHP

SIZE: 10 million km²
POPULATION: 746 million
NUMBER OF COUNTRIES: 44

While it's one of the smallest continents, Europe is still heavily populated, home to around one in ten people on Earth.

ASIA

HOW YOU PRONOUNCE MY NAME AY-ZHUH

SIZE: 44.58 million km²
POPULATION: 4.56 billion
NUMBER OF COUNTRIES: 48

The world's largest continent is home to some of the world's most populated countries, including China and India.

AFRICA

HOW YOU PRONOUNCE MY NAME A-FRUH-KUH

SIZE: 30 million km²
POPULATION: 1.27 billion
NUMBER OF COUNTRIES: 54

On top of a diverse climate and wildlife, this continent has more countries than any other, including Egypt, Nigeria and South Africa.

OCEANIA

HOW YOU PRONOUNCE MY NAME OW-SHEE-AA-NEE-UH

SIZE: 8.5 million km²
POPULATION: 41.5 million
NUMBER OF COUNTRIES: 14

This region is made up of Australia and 1,000 islands, including New Zealand and Papa New Guinea.

ANTARCTICA

HOW YOU PRONOUNCE MY NAME AN-TAAK-TUH-KUH

SIZE: 14.2 million km²
POPULATION: 1,000-5,000
NUMBER OF COUNTRIES: 0

There are no permanent settlements in this icy wilderness, except research stations used by visiting scientists.

WATCH THIS!

TAKE THE WORLD QUIZ!

SCAN WITH YOUR PHONE OR TABLET

https://bit.ly/3p7Fcsg

© Getty

AFRICA

Africa is the hottest continent. The world's highest temperature of 58°C was recorded in Libya. This is one of ten countries in the Sahara, which is the largest hot desert in the world. But Africa isn't all sand dunes; you'll find a range of climates and biomes here.

The continent is evenly split between the Northern and Southern Hemispheres. Unusually, this means Africa has opposite climates at any time of the year, so when it's summer in one part, it's winter in the other. Meanwhile, it's warm and wet all year round on the Equator, which are perfect conditions for the Congo Rainforest. Second largest after the Amazon, the Congo contains 10,000 species of tropical plants and endangered animals. This includes great apes like bonobos, chimpanzees and both lowland and mountain gorillas.

Both the Tropics of Cancer and Capricorn also intersect with Africa. Around these regions, you'll find the wide open grasslands known as savannah, the most famous of which is the Serengeti in Tanzania. Every year, tourists go on safari here to marvel at the wildlife. Some of the biggest attractions include elephants, giraffes, zebras, rhinos, hippos, lions and cheetahs. Africa is also home to another amazing animal:

humanity. The continent is the second most populous, with more than a billion people. Algeria is Africa's largest country by size, while Nigeria has the biggest population. Other major countries include Egypt, Libya and Morocco in the north; Angola and the Democratic Republic of Congo in central Africa; Ethiopia, Kenya and Mozambique in the east; and Ghana, Mali and Niger in the west, plus, Botswana and South Africa – surprise, surprise – in the south. Africa also includes the island nations of the Seychelles and Madagascar in the Indian Ocean, as well as Cape Verde and St Helena in the Atlantic.

LION

HOW YOU PRONOUNCE MY NAME

LAI-UHN

Though often called the 'king of the jungle', lions actually reside on Africa's vast savannah, where they live and hunt together in groups.

MOUNT KILIMANJARO

HOW YOU PRONOUNCE MY NAME MOWNT KI-LUH-MUHN-JAA-ROW

Located in Tanzania, Africa's tallest mountain at 5,895 metres isn't part of a mountain range. Instead, it stands alone looming over the wild plains.

PYRAMID PUZZLE

Ancient Egyptians often built mazes inside their pyramids to protect the Pharaoh's mummy and his treasures from tomb robbers. Can you find your way from one end to the other?

Africa is an incredibly diverse place. It is has almost 3,000 different ethnic groups, many with their own languages and traditions, so it's common for countries to speak several languages and belong to different groups.

The north is also largely Arabic, while some descendants of white Europeans who established colonies in Africa in the 19th century live in the south. There's also a large Indian community in East Africa. As a result, religion in Africa is largely split between Muslims in the north and Christians in the south, though some people also follow indigenous religions.

Three in every five Africans are under 25 years old. This makes the continent a lot younger than the rest of the world, but it still has a long history. Scientists believe that humans first evolved in Africa more than a million years ago. The oldest human fossils – as well as those of our ancestors – have been found in Ethiopia and South Africa.

The Ancient Egyptians formed one of the world's earliest civilisations nearly 5,000 years ago, building the Great Pyramids of Giza, while the kingdom of Carthage was one of Ancient Rome's greatest rivals, with its leader Hannibal invading Italy with war elephants in 218 BCE. During the middle ages, the Ghana, Mali and Songhai empires all flourished in western Africa. However, the slave trade from the 16th to 19th centuries had a devastating effect on the continent, with 12 million people forced to go work in the Americas.

While cities like Lagos and Kinshasa are expanding rapidly and countries like South Africa are becoming increasingly industrialised, most Africans live in the countryside. Farming is also the main industry, especially growing cotton, coffee and cocoa – the main ingredient in chocolate – to sell abroad. Mining is also big business, from digging for gold and diamonds to drilling for oil.

WATCH THIS!
GO ON A SAFARI!
SCAN WITH YOUR PHONE OR TABLET
https://bit.ly/3AbvzPC

STATS

POPULATION: 1.4 billion
LANGUAGES: Arabic, English, French, Portuguese, Swahili, Yoruba
LARGEST CITIES:
1. Cairo, Egypt
2. Lagos, Nigeria
3. Johannesburg, South Africa
4. Kinshasa, DR Congo
5. Luanda, Angola
SIZE: 30 million km²

LAGOS, NIGERIA

 HOW YOU PRONOUNCE MY NAME

LAY-GOS, NAI-JEEUH-REE-UH

Every hour, 77 people move here seeking a better life, making it one of the fastest-growing cities in the world.

KANGA/ KHANGA

 HOW YOU PRONOUNCE MY NAME

KANG-GUH

A traditional East African outfit, this brightly coloured cloth can be worn as a skirt, head-wrap, apron and in lots of other ways.

KINSHASA, DEMOCRATIC REPUBLIC OF CONGO

 HOW YOU PRONOUNCE MY NAME

KIN-SHAA-SUH, DEH-MUH-KRA-TUHK RUH-PUH-BLUHK UHV KONG-GOW

More people speak French in this sprawling capital on the banks of the River Congo than in any other city.

NAIROBI, KENYA

HOW YOU PRONOUNCE MY NAME NAI-ROW-BEE, KEH-NYUH

This capital city has a national park in the middle of it, where lions, giraffes and rare black rhino roam freely.

JOHANNESBURG, SOUTH AFRICA

HOW YOU PRONOUNCE MY NAME JOW-HA-NUHS-BUHG, SOWTH A-FRUH-KUH

Nicknamed 'Joburg', this thriving city is full of skyscrapers, including Africa's tallest building, the 269m-high Hillbrow Tower.

AFRICAN ELEPHANT

HOW YOU PRONOUNCE MY NAME A-FRUH-KUHN EH-LUH-FNT

The world's largest land mammal, a male elephant reaches up to 3m in height and weighs up to 6 tonnes – that's three times heavier than a car!

© Getty

ASIA

Asia is massive. The largest of all the continents, it covers one third of all the land on Earth. You'd take in every kind of climate travelling from the icy Siberian tundra in the north to the warm, wet rainforests near the Equator. It's bordered by three oceans: the Arctic to the north, Pacific to the east, and Indian to the south.

But Asia's not just a big place; it's also full of big things. Here you can find Everest, the tallest mountain – plus the next hundred highest peaks in the world. At the other end of the spectrum, it has got the world's deepest lake, Lake Baikal – plus the largest

in the Caspian Sea. It's not just the natural world that's super-sized: Tokyo is the planet's largest city, Hong Kong has more skyscrapers than anywhere else and the Great Wall of China is the longest human-made structure.

As Asia is so big and diverse, it's often talked about in terms of regions. With this in mind, we're going to cover the areas known as the Middle East and Southeast Asia in different parts of this book. But that still leaves lots to talk about: this section will cover the enormous nations of China and India, both of which have a billion citizens

each. That's a lot of people – more than all of North America! You'll also find major countries like Afghanistan, Pakistan and Nepal in the south, which are spread over the mountain ranges of the Hindu Kush and the Himalayas. On the east coast, you'll find the neon-lit skyscraper cities of Japan and South Korea, where the world's electronics are invented. Plus, meet the camel-riding nomads of Mongolia and Kazakhstan in the landlocked centre of the continent. These countries are home to some of the world's oldest civilisations, and they continue to have a lot of influence.

SUSHI

  HOW YOU PRONOUNCE MY NAME — SOO-SHEE

While seafood is popular in East Asia, these bundles of fish – often served raw – wrapped in vinegared rice are uniquely Japanese.

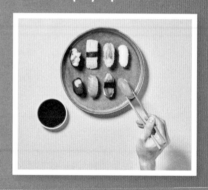

THE FORBIDDEN CITY

 HOW YOU PRONOUNCE MY NAME — FUH-BI-DUHN SI-TEE

This giant palace in the heart of Beijing contains about 9,000 rooms and belonged to the Chinese emperors during the Ming and Qing dynasties.

NUR-SULTAN, KAZAKHSTAN

 HOW YOU PRONOUNCE MY NAME — NUR-SUL-TAN, KA-ZUHK-STAAN

This capital is named after Kazakhstan's first president, who spent vast sums of the country's oil profits turning the city into an architectural wonder.

COLOUR IN THE PANDA

Great pandas are famous for their monochrome markings. Living in the mountain forests of southwestern China, their white fur helps them hide during snowy winter, while their black face, neck arms and legs let them blend in with the shadows during summer.

USING THE PHOTOGRAPH, COLOUR IN THE DRAWING OF THE CUTE PANDA!

MUMBAI, INDIA

 HOW YOU PRONOUNCE MY NAME MUM-BAI, IND-EE-UH

India's biggest city has 12 million people and is the headquarters for the country's famous Bollywood film industry.

BENGAL TIGER

 HOW YOU PRONOUNCE MY NAME BEN-GAWL TAI-GUH

Living in the subtropical jungles of India, Bangladesh, Nepal and Bhutan, this big cat's stripes help it blend in with the tall grass.

There are more people in Asia than all the other continents combined. That means there are lots of different groups of people, often in the same country, while countries can be very different from one side of the continent to the other.

There are 2,300 languages in Asia. The most spoken language is Chinese simply because there are more Chinese people. But there are several Chinese dialects that are spoken in different regions. Mandarin, which is spoken in Beijing, is the country's official language.

Hindi is the second most spoken language for the same reason: India is very big. But Hindi isn't the only language Indians speak; the country has 23 recognised languages. Many of these are regional – for instance, Punjabi is spoken in Punjab. Some are also shared with other countries: Pakistan also uses Urdu and Bangladesh speaks Bengali. As well as speaking multiple tongues, there are also multiple alphabets. While most of the world uses the Latin alphabet, throughout South and East Asia many countries have their own way of writing.

Religion also varies. More than 80 per cent of Indians are Hindu. Buddhism, Sikhism and Jainism all began there too. Pakistan is the second largest Muslim country, and neighbouring Afghanistan and much of Central Asia are mostly Muslim too. People in Japan are almost evenly split between Buddhism and Shintoism. Most South Koreans say they don't have a religion, while communist countries North Korea and China are officially atheist.

Asian art and culture has inspired the world for centuries – from Chinese ceramics and Japanese woodblock to Afghan rugs. Today, India is the world's largest film producer, making more than 2,500 a year. South Korean pop music, nicknamed K-pop, is soaring up the charts worldwide, and Chinese social network TikTok is being downloaded on every phone.

TAJ MAHAL

HOW YOU PRONOUNCE MY NAME

TAAJ MUH-HALL

This immense white marble mausoleum was built in the Indian city of Agra by Mughal Emperor Shah Jahan in memory of his wife in the 17th Century.

SEOUL, SOUTH KOREA

HOW YOU PRONOUNCE MY NAME

SOWL, SOWTH KUH-REE-UH

Meaning 'Capital' in Korean, Seoul is home to 26 million people – half the country's population.

STATS

POPULATION: 4.6 billion
LANGUAGES: Mandarin, Cantonese, Hindi, Punjabi, Bangla, Japanese, Korean
LARGEST CITIES:
1. Tokyo, Japan
2. Shanghai, China
3. Mumbai, India
4. Dhaka, Bangladesh
5. Karachi, Pakistan
SIZE: 44.5 million km²

BEIJING, CHINA

 HOW YOU PRONOUNCE MY NAME BAY-JING, CHAI-NUH

This capital in northern China is the only city in the world that has hosted both the summer and winter Olympics.

KING COBRA

 HOW YOU PRONOUNCE MY NAME KING KOW-BRUH

This snake, which grows up to five metres long and has a venomous bite strong enough to kill an elephant, lives in north India and southern China.

TOKYO, JAPAN

 HOW YOU PRONOUNCE MY NAME TO-KEE-O, JUH-PAN

This mega-city of 39 million people is three times as big as London on an island that's roughly the same size as Great Britain.

DALAI LAMA

 HOW YOU PRONOUNCE MY NAME DA-LAI LAA-MUH

The head monk of Tibetan Buddhism has traditionally governed the region of Tibet in the Himalayas, but has lived in exile since China took control.

CRICKET

 HOW YOU PRONOUNCE MY NAME KRI-KUHT

Introduced by the British during their colonial rule, this bat-and-ball game is the most popular sport in India and Pakistan.

© Getty

45

CENTRAL AMERICA & THE CARIBBEAN

North America is much more than the continental mainland. It's also home to Central America, a narrow strip of land that bridges the Americas, joining North and South together. This region is also surrounded by water, with the Pacific Ocean to the west and the Caribbean Sea to the east, while the Caribbean itself is full of amazing islands.

There are seven countries in Central America: Belize, Guatemala, El Salvador and Honduras in the north, plus Nicaragua, Costa Rica and Panama in the south. Nicaragua is the largest, while Guatemala is the most populous. Panama is perhaps the most famous for its huge human-made waterway. The Panama Canal offers ships a shortcut between the Pacific and Caribbean so they don't have to sail around South America.

There are 30 inhabited islands in the Caribbean. The largest are Cuba, Hispaniola, Jamaica and Puerto Rico. While Cuba and Jamaica are countries, Hispaniola is shared by two nations: Haiti and the Dominican Republic. Meanwhile, Puerto Rico is part of the United States. They are all popular travel destinations, with the region attracting 30 million tourists a year.

Both Central America and the Caribbean lie between the Tropic of Cancer and the Equator. This means that the temperature is warm all year round, but there can be a lot of storms in the summer. The Caribbean is mostly flat, while Central America is mountainous, with active volcanoes all the way down its west coast. Both regions are covered in rainforests, which are full of monkeys, parrots and big cats like jaguars and pumas. They also have white, sandy beaches and coral reefs that offer snorkellers views of sea turtles, manatees and manta rays. The farmers there grow crops that they sell around the world, including coffee, bananas and sugarcane.

DID YOU KNOW?

While only 30 are inhabited, the Caribbean is made up of 7,000 islands.

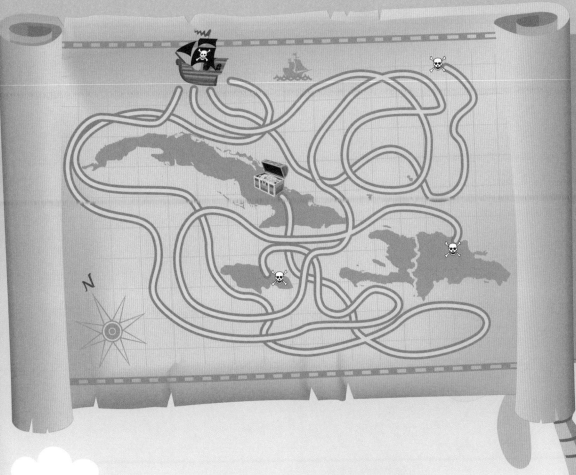

THE TREASURE MAP MAZE

In the late 17th Century, the Caribbean was famous for pirates. Help this pirate find his treasure to discover which ports were the most popular with buccaneers.

ANSWER:

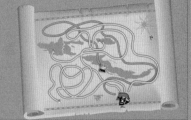

ARENAL VOLCANO

HOW YOU PRONOUNCE MY NAME A-REH-NAL VOL-KAY-NOW

This volcano in Costa Rica is one of the region's most active, erupting almost nonstop from 1968 until 2010. It still regularly smokes and rumbles.

GUATEMALA CITY, GUATEMALA

HOW YOU PRONOUNCE MY NAME GWA-TUH-MAA-LUH SI-TEE

More than 3 million people live in the largest city in Central America, which is high in the mountains and surrounded by volcanoes.

THREE-TOED SLOTH

HOW YOU PRONOUNCE MY NAME THREE-TOWD SLOTH

The world's slowest mammal hangs out in Central America's rainforests, where they sleep 15 hours a day and barely move more than 37m.

HAVANA, CUBA

 HOW YOU PRONOUNCE MY NAME HUH-VA-NUH, KYOO-BUH

The colourful capital of the Caribbean's largest island is a tourist hotspot, famous for its nightlife and art scene.

KINGSTON, JAMAICA

 HOW YOU PRONOUNCE MY NAME KINGS-TN, JUH-MAY-KUH

One in three Jamicians live in the island's capital, which is also the largest English-speaking city south of the United States.

DID YOU KNOW?

Belize is the least populated Central American country with less than 500,000 people.

PANAMA CITY, PANAMA

 HOW YOU PRONOUNCE MY NAME PA-NUH-MAA SI-TEE, PA-NUH-MAA

Thanks to the nearby canal bringing in lots of business, Panama's capital is a hustling, bustling financial hub.

KEEL-BILLED TOUCAN

HOW YOU PRONOUNCE MY NAME
KEEL-BILD TOO-KN

The national bird of Belize can be found throughout Central America. Its great, big rainbow-coloured bill makes up around one third of its body size.

SANTO DOMINGO, DOMINICAN REPUBLIC

HOW YOU PRONOUNCE MY NAME
SAN-TOW DUH-MING-GOW, DUH-MI-NUH-KUHN RUH-PUH-BLUHK

The Caribbean's biggest city is also the oldest European settlement in the Americas, founded in 1496 by Christopher Columbus' younger brother, Bartholomew.

WATCH THIS!

EXPLORE THE GREAT BARRIER REEF

SCAN WITH YOUR PHONE OR TABLET

https://bit.ly/3dhX1Co

ANDROS BARRIER REEF

HOW YOU PRONOUNCE MY NAME
AN-DROS BA-REE-UH REEF

At 225km long, this coral reef in the Bahamas is one of the world's longest. It's a habitat for parrotfish, red snappers, green turtles and more.

You can travel throughout most of Central America and only need to speak one language: Spanish. It's the official language of every country except Belize, which speaks English. However, many people in the region also speak indigenous languages. This is because three in five have a mix of Native American and European heritage.

This includes the Maya, who built a great civilisation that flourished between 250-900 CE. They had cities across modern-day Mexico, Belize, Guatemala and Honduras. A few lasted until the 16th century and were taken over when the Spanish invaded. While the Native Americans were oppressed for a long time, today many people proudly celebrate their roots.

The Caribbean islands are more varied. While Spain colonised Cuba, Puerto Rico and half of Hispaniola, they weren't the only Europeans in the region. The British ruled Jamaica, the Bahamas, Trinidad and Tobago, as well as many smaller islands. The French governed modern-day Haiti, while the Dutch and Danish had colonies too, so today the islands speak a mix of European languages. But most are actually descended from West Africans taken as slaves to work on the islands, rather than Europeans.

This fusion of Native American, African and Spanish influences has given Cuba a lively culture. It has got the whole world dancing with the invention of salsa and rumba, as well as the cha-cha and conga. The country is also unique in that it's only one of five in the world that is communist.

When most people think of Jamaica, they think of reggae music. The most famous reggae star was Bob Marley, who also drew attention to the popular Jamaican religion, rastafarianism. Rastas believe that Haile Selassie, the Emperor of Ethiopia from 1930 to 1974, was their saviour. They also grow their hair in dreadlocks, believing it shouldn't be cut, and wear clothing in red, gold and green – the colours of the Ethiopian flag.

STATS

POPULATION: 96 million
LANGUAGES: Spanish, English, French, Mesoamerican indigenous languages, Creole
LARGEST CITIES:
1. Guatemala City, Guatemala
2. Santo Domingo, Dominican Republic
3. Port-au-Prince, Haiti
4. San Salvador, El Salvador
5. San Juan, Puerto Rico, United States
SIZE: 799,180 KM^2

© Getty

NORTH AMERICA

North America is the third largest continent in the world. It contains many more countries than just the United States of America and Canada. Indeed, there are 23 countries in total, including Mexico, Cuba, Guatemala, Haiti, the Dominican Republic and Honduras. There are also many islands associated with European nations such as the United Kingdom and France.

The continent has been inhabited for thousands of years, but its modern history began in 1492 when the explorer Christopher Columbus sailed from Spain and 'discovered' the land. There was a lot of tension and fighting between the indigenous Americans and the many Europeans who decided to move and settle there. This is when new nations such as the United States, Canada and Mexico began to form.

The largest North American country today is Canada (the second largest country in the world after Russia), followed by the United States. Mexico City in Mexico has the largest population of any city on the continent, while Greenland, which is on the North American tectonic plate, is the world's largest island. As you can imagine, it's a very diverse part of the world. As well as the cities, there are deserts, temperate forests, taiga, mountains and plains, as well as some huge lakes.

The climate is also varied. Canada has cold arctic air in the north. Henderson Lake in Vancouver, Canada is also the rainiest part of North America – 9,307mm of rain fell in 1997. But the temperature warms the further south in North America you go, and the climate gets drier towards the west. Indeed, the hottest and driest national park is Death Valley in Eastern California – North America's lowest point, 86 metres (282 feet) below sea level. It recorded an air temperature of 57°C (134°F) during the summer of 1913 – the highest in the world!

DISNEY

HOW YOU PRONOUNCE MY NAME DIS-NEY

Mickey Mouse lives in a different kind of world: Disney World! It opened more than 50 years ago in Florida.

FIND THE GUITARS!

Music is a very important part of Mexican culture. Two of the colourful Mexican guitars in this picture are the same. Can you identify which ones?

FIND TWO SAME GUITARS

NIAGARA FALLS

HOW YOU PRONOUNCE MY NAME — NAI-A-GRUH-FAWLZ

These three waterfalls in Ontario, Canada are so powerful that they can generate 4 million kilowatts of electricity!

MEXICO CITY

HOW YOU PRONOUNCE MY NAME — MEK-SUH-KOW-SI-TEE

Mexico's capital is located in the mountains and it's the largest North American city by population, with 9.2 million people!

LAKE SUPERIOR

HOW YOU PRONOUNCE MY NAME — LAYK SOO-PEEUH-REE-UH

The largest of the Great Lakes of North America, this is a huge body of freshwater that covers an area of 82,000 sq km (31,700 sq miles).

NEW YORK

HOW YOU PRONOUNCE MY NAME — NEW-YOR-K

The United States' largest city has the Empire State Building and the Statue of Liberty, but it isn't the US capital – that's Washington DC.

The diverse culture of North America has been influenced by almost every region in the world, and there are differences from country to country, as well as within different regions. The Western, Midwest, Southeast, Northeast and South United States, for example, have their own traditions and customs. But people in the United States (and Canada) still have much in common. Most people identify themselves as Christians, dress in a similar way and eat food that is typically American, such as hamburgers, potato chips and apple pie!

English is the first language of most people living in Canada and the United States (although French is spoken as a first language by 23 per cent of the Canadian population). Television and film is also very important – Hollywood is the centre of the world's movie industry – but there is a great love of theatre and the arts, too. Sport is taken seriously, but the United States is more interested in baseball, basketball, ice hockey and American football rather than soccer and cricket.

Go further south in North America and the situation changes. Spanish is the dominant language in Mexico, Cuba and the Dominican Republic, for example, and the culture in this part of the world is influenced by Spain, as well as indigenous groups such as the Mayan people. Each country has its own literature, musical tastes and cuisine. The most popular sport among many of the nations is soccer, and Mexico has a flourishing film industry that is popular among Spanish speakers and beyond.

The continent has some very unique animals as well. American bison is North America's largest land mammal and you can find many of them in Yellowstone National Park. The bald eagle has become the symbol of the United States, while the Cuban trogon is the national bird of Cuba. The United States also has the greatest number of dogs: a staggering 75.8 million of them!

LOS ANGELES

HOW YOU PRONOUNCE MY NAME
LOS-AN-GEL-EEZ

This iconic part of Los Angeles is Hollywood, where some of the world's biggest film studios are based!

GRIZZLY BEARS

HOW YOU PRONOUNCE MY NAME
GRIZ-LEE BEUH

Grizzlies are a North American subspecies of the brown bear. See them at Yellowstone National Park!

STATS

POPULATION: 576 million
LANGUAGES: English, Spanish, French, Dutch, Danish, Indigenous languages
LARGEST CITIES:
1. Mexico City, Mexico
2. New York, USA
3. Los Angeles, USA
4. Toronto, Canada
5. Chicago, USA
SIZE: 24.71 million km^2

HAVANA

HOW YOU PRONOUNCE MY NAME
HUH-VA-NUH

Cuba's capital was founded by Spanish explorers in 1515, and it has architecture that is similar to Spain.

MONTREAL

HOW YOU PRONOUNCE MY NAME

MON-TREE-AWL

Montreal in Canada is the second largest French-speaking city in the world – the first is Paris!

KENNEDY SPACE CENTRE

HOW YOU PRONOUNCE MY NAME

KEN-E-DEE SPAYS CEN-TER

In 1969, the US became the first country to put a man on the Moon. It's also home to NASA, the world's leading space agency.

SOUTH AMERICA

A total of 12 countries make up South America, the largest of which is Brazil. The continent also includes Argentina, Peru, Colombia, Bolivia, Venezuela, Chile, Paraguay, Ecuador, Guyana, Uruguay and Suriname. They make up a region that is generally hot and humid, although the continent has four climatic areas that are tropical, temperate, arid or cold.

Brazil is the largest of the South American countries, taking up more than half of the land. Its largest city is São Paulo, where 12.4 million people live, making it the fourth most populated city in the world! But there are other amazing cities, such as Recife, which is similar to Venice with its waterways and bridges.

The Amazon River flows through Brazil, having travelled through Peru. This river is the second longest in the world after the Nile in Egypt, and the largest river in the world by volume. Around 10 million live on the banks of the river, which also meanders through Ecuador, Colombia, Venezuela, Bolivia, Suriname and Guyana either direct or through tributaries.

Most of the river also flows through the Amazon Rainforest – the largest tropical rainforest in the world. It spans nine countries and contains 10 per cent of the world's wildlife. It also has about 16,000 species of trees and 2.5 million different insects. It plays a big role in helping to reduce the effects of climate change by converting carbon dioxide into oxygen.

But that's not all. South America also boasts the highest mountain: Aconcagua in Argentina. This is in the Andes mountain range, which is the highest of North and South America, and reaches a height of 6.961 metres (22,838 feet). The Andes is also the world's longest continental mountain range.

Yet South America has other remarkable features. In Bolivia, Salar de Uyuni is the world's largest salt flat. Left behind by evaporated prehistoric lakes, it contains 10 billion tonnes of salt. Let's explore some more!

SÃO PAULO

HOW YOU PRONOUNCE MY NAME

SOWN-POW-LOW

Brazil's most populous city has an impressive skyline of skyscrapers, but it's also known for its wet weather.

BUENOS AIRES

HOW YOU PRONOUNCE MY NAME

BWEH-NOS AI-RUHZ

The capital of Argentina has a huge number of book shops – more per person than any other city in the world!

CARNIVAL

HOW YOU PRONOUNCE MY NAME

KAA-NUH-VL

The Carnival in Rio de Janeiro is held every year and attracts more than 2 million people every day it's on!

SPOT THE DIFFERENCE

The toco toucan is found in the tropical forests of South America. Can you spot the 10 differences between these two pictures?

ANSWER:

55

South American culture is steeped in tradition. As well as being influenced by the culture of indigenous tribes, it absorbs the traditions of many immigrants. They settled in the continent after colonists came from Europe and took over the land. Most of those colonists were from Spain, which is why the Spanish language is so widely spoken in South America. Indeed, Spanish is the main language of Bolivia, Ecuador, Chile, Peru, Colombia, Paraguay, Uruguay, Venezuela and Argentina. Brazilian people speak Portuguese, and in Suriname, Dutch is the official language.

Among the main industries on the continent are agriculture, industry, forestry and mining. Brazil, for instance, is the world's largest producer of coffee, and South America also has many cacao plantations. You will likely love cacao – it's the base ingredient in chocolate. Yum! The continent also cultivates Brazil nuts and cashews, and grows fruits such as pineapple and avocado, which are then exported around the world. South America accounts for about 16 per cent of global goods exports.

Bad things happen, though. Brazil is the continent's largest cattle-producing company, but many trees in the Amazon Rainforest are chopped down to clear room for livestock. The land is also used to grow soy, but this reduces the amont of carbon dioxide being converted to oxygen. The Amazon rainforest is also home to 1,300 species of bird, 430 types of mammal and 3,000 types of fish, and these can be affected by deforestation too. It's why conservationists are trying to protect the rainforest.

But it's not all serious! South Americans love to express themselves, and nowhere is that better seen that in Rio de Janeiro. Brazil's capital is well known for its colourful carnival, which mixes parades with music and dance. South Americans also love theatre and sport. Football is huge and some of the countries – notably Brazil and Argentina – are very successful.

FOOTBALL

 FOOT-BALL

Football is huge in South America. Brazil is the most successful World Cup-winning team, with five victories.

BOGOTÁ

 BOW-GUH-TAA

Bogotá is the capital of Colombia. Most of the world's emeralds originate from there.

AMAZON RAINFOREST

 A-MUH-ZN RAYN-FO-RUHST

The Amazon Rainforest is so big, it's nearly the size of Australia. it would fit France 10 times!

ATACAMA DESERT

 A-TUH-KAA-MUH DES-ERT

The Atacama Desert, located between the Andes and the Chilean coast range, is one of the driest places on Earth.

ANGEL FALLS

 HOW YOU PRONOUNCE MY NAME   ANE-GEL FALLS

Angel Falls is the highest waterfall in the world. It falls from a height of 979 metres (3,212 feet).

FEATURE #5

CARNIVAL

 HOW YOU PRONOUNCE MY NAME   KAA-NUH-VL

The Carnival in Rio de Janeiro is held ever year, and it attracts more than 2 million people every day!

STATS

POPULATION: 422.5 million
LANGUAGES: Spanish, Portuguese, English, Dutch, French, Aymara, Guarani, Quechua
LARGEST CITIES:
1. São Paulo, Brazil
2. Buenos Aires, Argentina
3. Rio de Janeiro, Brazil
4. Bogotá, Colombia
5. Lima, Peru
SIZE: 17.8 million km²

RIO DE JANEIRO

 HOW YOU PRONOUNCE MY NAME   REE-O DE JAN-AIR-O

The capital of Brazil is where you will find the impressive art deco statue, Christ the Redeemer, as well as an amazing carnival!

© Getty

EUROPE

While Europe is one of the smallest continents, it has had a huge impact. The Roman Empire, the Renaissance, the Enlightenment, the Industrial Revolution – all of these major historical events, which created beautiful works of art, spurred on science and invented democracy, started here and then spread around the world.

Europe also has people more than you might expect, with the third largest population after Asia and Africa. While that makes the continent a bit of a squeeze, Europeans live in some incredible places. You can see paintings, statues and more in the world's largest art gallery in Paris, enjoy

a masked carnvial along Venice's canals, then ride a dog sled through snowy Lapland. It's no wonder Europe's the most visited continent in the world, with half of all tourists going there on holiday.

The continent is located in the Northern Hemisphere. Countries like France and Germany in western Europe have a temperate climate, while eastern Europe – which includes the Czech Republic and Ukraine – is largely landlocked, so its winters are harsher and summers warmer. The winter is long and dark in the far north, which includes Finland and Sweden, while Greece and Spain in the south have hot, dry summers and mild winters.

More than half of Europe is made up of flat, low plains. The highest mountains are all located in the south. The Alps stretch across eight countries, while the Pyrenees divide France and Spain. The Urals in Russia acts as Europe's eastern border with Asia. The range also includes Europe's tallest peak, the 5,642 metre-high Mount Elbrus.

Europe is surrounded by the Mediterranean Sea to the south, the Arctic Ocean to the north, and the Atlantic Ocean to the West. In these waters, you will find Europe's five island nations: Cyprus, Iceland, Ireland, Malta and the United Kingdom (UK).

MATCH THE MONUMENTS

Where can you find these European landmarks? Match them up!

BRANDENBURG GATE, BERLIN **BIG BEN, LONDON** **ACROPOLIS, ATHENS** **KREMLIN, MOSCOW**

RUSSIA **GREECE** **GERMANY** **UNITED KINGDOM**

ANSWERS: 1. Brandenburg Gate - Germany, 2. Big Ben - United Kingdom, 3. Acropolis - Greece, 4. Kremlin - Russia

THE PRIME MERIDIAN

The Prime Meridian is the name given to the line of 0 longitude. This is the starting point for measuring distance both east and west around Earth. While this could have been anywhere, there is an international agreement that it runs through the Royal Observatory in Greenwich, England. This helps to make sure that all maps and charts look the same and are easier to read. The Prime Meridian also sets the standard for the world's 24 time zones, so every other time zone set its clock up to 12 hours ahead or 11 hours behind Greenwich.

59

PAELLA

 HOW YOU PRONOUNCE MY NAME PAI-EH-LUH

This popular rice dish from Spain is cooked over an open fire in a specially designed pan, which is shallow with side handles.

IRELAND

 HOW YOU PRONOUNCE MY NAME AI-UH-LUHND

Europe's second largest island is nicknamed the 'Emerald Isle' because of its green, rolling hills.

FRANCE

 HOW YOU PRONOUNCE MY NAME FRAANS

With vibrant cities, sunny beaches and mountains you can ski on, it's no wonder that France is Europe's most popular travel destination.

ATLANTIC PUFFIN

HOW YOU PRONOUNCE MY NAME
UHT-LAN-TUHK PUH-FN

Thousands of these fish-loving seabirds live in colonies along the coast of Iceland, as well as in France, the UK and Norway.

CLOGS

HOW YOU PRONOUNCE MY NAME
KLOG

These wooden shoes have been worn in the Netherlands since medival times. They are less popular now, but some farmers still prefer them to steel-capped boots.

Europe is home to some of the most widely spoken languages in the world. English is spoken in both the UK and Ireland, while many Europeans also speak English as a second language. In France and Monaco they speak French, and in Germany, Austria and Liechtenstein they speak German, while Belgium and Luxembourg speak both French and German, and Switzerland speaks French, German and Italian. Beyond Russia, Russian is spoken in Belarus, Poland and Ukraine. There are also lots of other national languages, and many Europeans countries also have languages only spoken in particular. For instance, Catalan, Valencian, Galician and Basque are spoken in different parts of Spain.

Some form of Christianity is the main religion in every European country. Austria, Belgium, France, Hungary, Portugal, Poland and Spain are mostly Roman Catholic. Scandinavia, the United Kingdom and the Netherlands are Protestant, while Eastern Orthodox Christians mainly live in Cyprus, Greece, Russia, Serbia and many other parts of Eastern Europe. Muslims also live in many European countries and form the majority in Albania, Bosnia and Herzegovina, as well as Turkey. Jewish people also live throughout Europe.

Though wealth varies between countries, Europe is one of the richest continents. Most people work in shops, hotels, restaurants or in offices providing other services, while many European companies rely on Asian companies to manufacture their products, there are still lots of factories. These make everything from chemicals to cars, including big names like Volkswagen, BMW, Ferrari and Fiat. European farms also grow most of the world's rye, more than half of the oats, and more than a third of the potatoes and wheat. Europe is a world leader in education and health. Governments generally provide healthcare to all citizens, so Europeans, on average, live longer than people in many other parts of the world.

STATS

POPULATION: 746 million
LANGUAGES: English, French, German, Russian, Italian, Polish
LARGEST CITIES:
1. Istanbul, Turkey
2. Moscow, Russia
3. London, UK
4. Berlin, Germany
5. Madrid, Spain
SIZE: 10 million km²

VATICAN CITY

HOW YOU PRONOUNCE MY NAME
VA-TUH-KUHN SI-TEE

The world's smallest country is less than 500m² and governed by the Pope, the head of the Catholic Church.

EUROPEAN UNION: NEW WORLD ORDER

After World War II ended in 1945, most countries fell into two groups. These were the communist countries of Eastern Europe led by Russia, known as the Soviet Union, and the democracies of Western Europe. There was an intense rivalry between the two sides and travel was restricted.

But in the early '90s, the Soviet Union broke apart, while Western Europe formed a new organisation called the European Union (EU). This allowed people in member states to live and work freely in each others countries.

Since 2004, 11 Eastern European countries have joined the EU. Many have even switched to a shared currency and combined military forces, making the continent more closely united.

EURSIAN LYNX

HOW YOU PRONOUNCE MY NAME

YUOR-RAY-ZHUHN LINGKS

This wild cat can only be found in Scandanavia and the Carpathian mountains, but there are conservation projects across Europe trying to boost their numbers.

FINLAND

HOW YOU PRONOUNCE MY NAME

FIN-LUHND

Finland has more forest than any other European country – trees cover 74 per cent of the country – an area larger than Italy.

GREECE

HOW YOU PRONOUNCE MY NAME

GREES

Democracy was invented in modern Greece's capital city all the way back in the 5th Century BCE.

RUSSIA

HOW YOU PRONOUNCE MY NAME RUH-SHUH

The world's largest country is so big it's in both Europe and Asia, though Russia's capital, Moscow, is in the west.

RIVER VOLGA

HOW YOU PRONOUNCE MY NAME RI-VUH VOL-GUH

Europe's longest river is the Volga in Russia. It stretches from its source north of Moscow for 3,531km, emptying into the Caspian Sea.

POLAND

HOW YOU PRONOUNCE MY NAME PO-LUHND

Here you'll find the world's largest castle, Malbork, which was a royal holiday home until Poland became a republic in 1918.

WHERE IS IT?

MIDDLE EAST

The Middle East is not a continent. Rather, it's a mix of countries from Africa, Central Asia, Southern Asia and Europe. It got its name 'Middle East' some time in the 19th century when people in the British Empire used the phrases 'Near East' and 'Far East' to describe parts of Asia. The area is very diverse, but most Middle East countries are Arab nations.

One of those – Qatar – was picked to host the 2022 World Cup. This tournament had to be moved to December because temperatures in the Middle East during the summer – when the event should have been held – are unbearably hot and dry. But even in the winter, the Middle East has a warm desert climate. In fact, it only has two seasons – there is no spring or autumn.

So which countries are included? The general understanding is that there are 18 countries in total. These are – deep breath – Bahrain, Cyprus, Egypt, Iran, Iraq, Israel, Jordan, Kuwait, Lebanon, Oman, Palestine, Qatar, Saudi Arabia, the Syrian Arab Republic, Turkey, the United Arab Emirates and Yemen.

The region also has many bodies of water, including the Mediterranean Sea, Red Sea, Arabian Sea, Caspian Sea, Indian Ocean, Gulf of Eden, Black Sea, Dead Sea and Persian Gulf. Even so, a lot of the region is desert, notably the Sahara, Arabian, Sinai, Libyan and Nubian! Rainfall is under 250mm per year in these parts and there is no vegetation – just sand and rocks.

Yet the deserts do contain lots of liquid: oil! This has made much of the region wealthy, with Saudi Arabia, Iran, Iraq, Kuwait and Libya having vast oil reserves as well as natural gas. Some states use their wealth to create stunning buildings and to invest in other countries around the world.

STATS

POPULATION: 411 million
LANGUAGES: Arabic, Hebrew, Kurdish, Persian and Turkish
LARGEST CITIES:
1. Cairo, Egypt
2. Tehran, Iran
3. Istanbul, Turkey
4. Baghdad, Iraq
5 Riyadh, Saudi Arabia
SIZE: 7,207,574 km^2

RELIGION

 HOW YOU PRONOUNCE MY NAME   RUH-LI-JN

Most of the Middle East's population follow Islam. Muslims must make a pilgrimage to Mecca in Saudi Arabia.

WATCH THIS!
THE MIDDLE EAST

SCAN WITH YOUR PHONE OR TABLET
https://bit.ly/3zH9lng

HUMMUS

 HOW YOU PRONOUNCE MY NAME HU-MUHS

Hummus is just one of the many delicious foods of the Middle East and along with the pizza-like mannakeesh, grilled halloumi and falafel.

TEHRAN

 HOW YOU PRONOUNCE MY NAME TEUH-RAAN

Tehran is the capital of Iran and has a population of 8.7 million. The Milad Tower located there is the sixth tallest tower in the world.

DID YOU KNOW?

The Middle East is where many religions originated.

THIRSTY WORK!

Arabian camels have one hump, which can store up to 80 pounds of fat and have been used for centuries for transport and war. Their wool can also be woven into cloth and their milk can be drunk. They are highly valued animals!

THIS CAMEL HAS GOT THE HUMP BECAUSE HE'S THIRSTY. CAN YOU LEAD HIM TO WATER?

ISTANBUL

 HOW YOU PRONOUNCE MY NAME I-STAN-BUL

Turkey's largest city with 13 million people, is actually in two continents: Europe and Asia. It has the largest covered market in the world.

WORD JUMBLE

Below are some countries that have had their letters mixed up. Can you rearrange them to find the correct names?

NIRBAHA

TWKUIA

TPAELENIS

RTQAA

RYSAI

MEENY

ANSWERS: BAHRAIN, KUWAIT, PALESTINE, QATAR, SYRIA, YEMEN

CAIRO

 KAY-RO

Egypt's capital city is by far the largest – more than 10 million people live there! Located by the River Nile, it's the site of the Great Pyramid of Giza.

Of the 18 countries in the Middle East, 13 of them are Arab nations. People who live in these countries speak Arabic as their first language, but Persian, Turkish, Berber and Kurdish are also spoken in the region. Most, but not all, Arabs also follow Islam. Yet Cyprus is mainly Christian, and Christianity is practiced in some other parts of the Middle East, while Israel follows Judaism.

Religion and tradition are really important. There are dress codes in many Middle Eastern countries and Muslims are expected to dress modestly. Women may wear a hijab or khimar, for example, and men may dress in a long robe and a head covering. Rules and customs differ depending on the country, and some, such as in Iran and Saudi Arabia, can be very strict. There are also things which women can't do that men can.

Sadly, the region has also been involved in many conflicts, and you may learn about them in the news.

These are often started because of various power struggles, although the wars have also involved countries from outside the region, such as the US and UK.

Yet there is great investment, too. As well as amazing ancient architecture – such as Petra in Jordan, where temples and tombs are carved directly into desert sandstone, or the ruins of the former capital of the Persian Empire, Persepolis in Iran – there are many great modern buildings, much of it paid for using the money made from selling oil.

The Burj Khalifa in Dubai in the United Arab Emirates is the tallest building in the world. The King Abdullah Petroleum Studies and Research Centre in Riyadh, Saudi Arabia, looks like a spaceship! And the Sheikh Zayed Grand Mosque in Abu Dhabi mixes many architectural styles. One thing's for sure: the Middle East is an interesting part of the world.

BURQA

 HOW YOU PRONOUNCE MY NAME **BUH-KUH**

The burqa is a concealing Islamic veil that covers the face and body. It's one of a number of clothes worn by people in the Middle East.

BAGHDAD

HOW YOU PRONOUNCE MY NAME **BAG-DAD**

Iraq's capital is home to 7 million people, and it's one of the hottest cities in the world. Sadly, a lot of its treasures have been destroyed by war.

DUBAI

 HOW YOU PRONOUNCE MY NAME **DOO-BAI**

Dubai is a popular city for tourists today, but it was mostly desert only 20 years ago. It has the tallest building in the world!

DID YOU KNOW?

Half of the world's petrol is found in the Middle East.

RIYADH

 HOW YOU PRONOUNCE MY NAME **MOWNT EH-RUH-BUHS**

The capital of Saudi Arabia is located on the Arabian Peninsula. Its tallest skyscraper looks like it has a handle on top!

SOUTHEAST ASIA

There are 11 countries in Southeast Asia – a region that lies just below China. These are Indonesia, Singapore, Cambodia, Malaysia, East Timor, Myanmar, Vietnam, Thailand, Laos, Brunei and the Philippines. Many of the countries are located on the Asian mainland, but a good number are made up of islands. Indonesia, for example, consists of more than 17,000 islands, and there are 25,000 across the region! Ferries and flights help people to get around.

The region is also very warm and humid. Temperatures tend to range between 25C and 35C all year round, but most of the countries also experience wet seasons. Usually beginning around May and ending in October, the region is pounded by heavy bursts of rain called monsoons. They bring relief after the hot summer months and help with agriculture, but can cause floods that wash away homes and devastate rice fields.

Agriculture is important to the region's economy. As well as a mix of lowlands and uplands, rivers and forests, there are fertile plains that are ideal for the cultivation of rice. Corn, wheat, soybean, palm oil and sugarcane are also staple crops and cotton is grown in some countries for use in making clothes and other garments. The long coastlines and warm, shallow oceans provide access to the sea and provide a great environment for fishing.

Tourists flock to Southeast Asia, too. There are lots of great beaches lapped by crystal clear waters, as well as many amazing sights. Aside from national parks where you can see limestone caves or Komodo dragons – the largest lizards in the world – there is a great deal of history on show, including the temple complex of Angkor Wat in Cambodia. There are many great modern cities too, some of which have burst into life over the last 100 years.

DOT-TO-DOT

Bring this Komodo dragon to life!

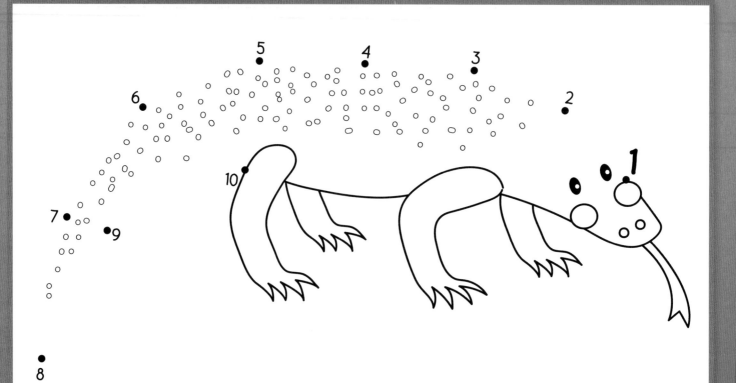

ORANGUTANS

 UR-RANG-UH-TAN

The Islands of Borneo and Sumatra are home to these great apes. Southeast Asia also contains other diverse animals, including the Sumatran rhino an Malayan tapir.

THAILAND

  TAI-LAND

Once known as Siam, Thailand is the world's largest exporter of rice. Its capital is Bangkok.

MUSLIMS

MUS-LIMS

There are around 240 million Muslims in Southeast Asia – that's about 42 per cent of the region's entire population.

Southeast Asia is a very diverse region, culturally and historically. There is great Indian and Chinese influence, but each country has its own traditions and unique ways of doing things. As well as hundreds of different ethnic groups, there are many religious beliefs. More than 1,200 languages are spoken (700 in Indonesia alone), but English is also common.

Most of the Southeast Asian population (about a fifth) live on Java, one of the Greater Sunda Islands in Indonesia. It is the most densely populated island in the world and it was mainly formed by volcanic eruptions. The Philippines, Vietnam, Thailand and Myanmar also have large populations. More than a third of those living in the region are below the age of 19.

Islam is the most widely practiced religion, especially in Indonesia, Malaysia and Brunei. Buddhism, Christianity, Hinduism and Animism are also practised and there are many places of worship across the region. In fact, in Thailand alone, where Buddhism is followed by 95 per cent of the population, there are 35,000 temples, while Angkor Wat in Cambodia is the largest religious monument in the world.

If you fancy something to eat and drink, there's plenty of choice, with a mix of street food and high-end restaurants and everything else in between. Popular ingredients include ginger, garlic, chilies, dried onions, soy, tofu and rice. Curries are common dishes and there is a lot of borrowing of ideas from each country's cuisine. Globally, Thai food is perhaps the most popular.

As the years have gone by, Southeast Asia has also moved with the times. Indonesia has the third largest number of Facebook users in the world (the Philippines are sixth and Vietnam is seventh). Indonesia has the second largest TikTok audience in the world and the third largest number of mobile phones in use. Southeast Asian people are very social!

LAOS

HOW YOU PRONOUNCE MY NAME **LOWS**

Laos is the only landlocked country in Southeast Asia and it is one of only five communist countries in the world.

STATS

POPULATION: 682 million
LANGUAGES: Lao, Thai, Burmese, Khmer, Vietnamese, Tagalog, Malay, Indonesian and Chinese dialects
LARGEST CITIES:
  1. Jakarta, Indonesia
  2. Manila, The Philippines
  3. Bangkok, Thailand
  4. Ho Chi Minh City, Vietnam
  5. Singapore
SIZE: 4.5 million km^2

SINGAPORE

 HOW YOU PRONOUNCE MY NAME **SING-UH-PAW**

One of the smallest countries in the world, Singapore is also a city-state – voted the cleanest and greenest of them all!

CAMBODIA

HOW YOU PRONOUNCE MY NAME

KAM-BOW-DEE-UH

Home to Angkor Wat, Cambodia has a very young population – the average age is just 26 years old.

RICE

HOW YOU PRONOUNCE MY NAME

RISE

Rice is the most important food in Southeast Asia, providing lots of calories while also making money through sales abroad.

BEACHES

HOW YOU PRONOUNCE MY NAME

BEE-CHIHZ

From Vietnam's Ha Long Bay to Bali, tourism is very important to the Southeast Asian region, and it's well known for its fabulous beaches.

INDONESIA

HOW YOU PRONOUNCE MY NAME

IN-DUH-NEE-ZEE-UH

Indonesia is home to 139 volcanoes, as well as the tallest island peak in the world, Puncak Jaya, which is 4,884 metres above sea level.

AUSTRALIA

Australia is the sixth largest country in the world. It is so big that it could cover almost all of Europe. It is also the only country that doubles as a continent. But not many people live there, considering its huge size! The country has a population of nearly 26 million people, yet by comparison, 746 million live in Europe.

Around 90 per cent of people in Australia also live on the coast in large, densely populated cities. It's not easy to live anywhere else because the rural parts – called the outback – are far too hot and dry. There are no rivers and very little water in the outback. Not much grows there,

and most of it is covered in Australia's largest deserts.

You may well have heard of some of the big cities in Australia, especially Sydney and Melbourne. But did you know that neither of these are the capital? That honour goes to Canberra, which is midway between them. Sydney and Melbourne are not the biggest cities by area either (even though they contain the most people). That would be Brisbane!

Yet that doesn't mean exploring the rest of Australia isn't exciting. There are six states in the country and, in the north-east state of Queensland, there are dense rainforests.

They include the Daintree, which is the world's oldest living tropical rainforest packed with unique plants and waterways.

Running parallel to the east coast is the Great Dividing Range. This is a series of mountains, plateaus and hills that stretch more than 3,500 kilometres (2,175 miles) and includes Australia's highest peak, Mount Kosciuszko, which is 2,220 metres (7,310 feet) high! In the centre of Australia is Uluru, a huge sandstone formation. It means Australia is richly diverse, with loads of fascinating natural and human-made creations to explore.

TRUE OR FALSE?

AUSTRALIA HAS HOSTED THE OLYMPIC GAMES TWICE
TRUE ☐ OR FALSE ☐

THERE ARE MORE THAN 750 SPECIES OF REPTILE IN AUSTRALIA
TRUE ☐ OR FALSE ☐

AUSTRALIA HAS A STRONG BILL OF RIGHTS
TRUE ☐ OR FALSE ☐

CANBERRA HAS ALWAYS BEEN THE AUSTRALIAN CAPITAL
TRUE ☐ OR FALSE ☐

THE BEST-BEHAVED CONVICTS BECAME OFFICERS IN THE FIRST AUSTRALIAN POLICE FORCE
TRUE ☐ OR FALSE ☐

ANSWERS: True, True, False, False, True

SYDNEY

HOW YOU PRONOUNCE MY NAME SID-NEE

The most populous city, Sydney, is the capital of New South Wales, and it boasts the stunning Harbour Bridge and Opera House.

KANGAROO

 HOW YOU PRONOUNCE MY NAME KANG-GUH-ROO

Kangaroos are perhaps the best-known of the Australian animals. They have powerful hind legs that allow them to very quickly bound across land.

MELBOURNE

  HOW YOU PRONOUNCE MY NAME MEL-BN

Located on the coast in the state of Victoria, Melbourne is best known for hosting the oldest and most-visited public art gallery in Australia.

KOALA

 HOW YOU PRONOUNCE MY NAME KOW-AA-LUH

Found in the eucalyptus forests in the east of Australia, koalas live solitary lifestyles and survive by eating leaves that are poisonous to most other animals.

DID YOU KNOW?

It would take you 27 years to visit every Australian beach for a day!

ULURU

  HOW YOU PRONOUNCE MY NAME OO-LUH-ROO

Located in the Northern Territory with the town of Alice Springs 450 kilometres (250 miles away), this sandstone rock is sacred to indigenous Australians.

For tens of thousands of years, the only humans living in the land that forms Australia were the aboriginal people. They migrated from Asia up to 60,000 years ago, and lived in small communities where they survived by hunting and gathering.

The situation began to change in 1606 when Dutch explorers 'discovered' the land. They could have taken it over, ruled the aboriginal population and encouraged people from the Netherlands to move there, but they decided it was too dry and unsuitable for this.

The British, however, had other ideas. They wanted to send their prisoners far, far away, so in 1788, Captain Arthur Phillip led 11 ships carrying 1,400 convicts, soldiers and free people to the other side of the world from Britain. They founded Australia and the settlements grew, although it led to fighting against the aboriginal people over who owned the land.

Today, the aboriginal culture and people are better protected and valued, but there is still some way to go. While the country is multicultural, the dominant culture is mainly Western – the British monarch is still the head of state! People enjoy lots of sports, including swimming, cricket, rugby, surfing, sailing and Australian rules football. They love cinema, theatre, music and literature.

Australia is also home to lots of wonderful wildlife. Since the country developed alone for many thousands of years, 80 per cent of the animals that inhabit the land are unique to Australia. You only find kangaroos, koalas, platypus and echidnas living natively there. But beware: danger also looms. The country has the most animals with deadly venom!

Watch out for the taipan, which is often called the world's most venomous snake. It's one of 20 types of snakes in Australia. There are dangerous spiders too, the worst being the Sydney funnel web, whose bite can kill within hours if not treated.

DINGO

HOW YOU PRONOUNCE MY NAME

DING-GOW

These large land predators are medium-sized dogs that live in the forests, plains, desert regions and mountainous rural areas of western and central Australia.

STATS

POPULATION: 25,690,000
LANGUAGES: English
LARGEST CITIES:
1. Sydney
2. Melbourne
3. Brisbane
4. Perth
5 Adelaide
SIZE: 7.692 million km^2

PERTH

HOW YOU PRONOUNCE MY NAME

PUHTH

Perth is in the state of Western Australia, where Aboriginal Australians lived for 45,000 years. It has 19 beaches within easy reach of the city.

SPOT THE DIFFERENCE

Can you spot the differences between the Australian animals in these two images?

DID YOU KNOW?

The Great Barrier Reef is the largest coral reef system in the world.

ANSWER:

WALLABY

WOMBAT

HOW YOU PRONOUNCE MY NAME WOM-BAT

Wombats are nocturnal animals who spend most of their days burrowed away underground. They can run at speeds of 40km/h (25mph).

HOW YOU PRONOUNCE MY NAME WO-LUH-BEE

They look like kangaroos – they even have pouches – but wallabies are actually smaller. Their young are called joeys.

BRISBANE

HOW YOU PRONOUNCE MY NAME BRIS-BIN

Brisbane is the capital of Queensland, and enjoys 280 days of sun each year. It's close to the Great Barrier Reef and Daintree Rainforest.

PLATYPUS

HOW YOU PRONOUNCE MY NAME PLA-TUH-PUHS

Platypuses are like a mash-up of animals with a bill, fur, tail and webbed feet. They are also venomous and lay eggs!

ADELAIDE

HOW YOU PRONOUNCE MY NAME A-DUH-LAYD

The capital of South Australia, Adelaide is known for its festivals and food, as well as some amazing historic architecture.

© Getty

WHERE IS IT?

THE ARCTIC

You may have already heard about the Arctic because it's the location of the North Pole, where Father Christmas lives. But did you know that the Arctic is also the world's northernmost continent and that the North Pole isn't actually on land? It's on ice-covered waters, and it's possible to travel underneath it! In 1958, a submarine called USS Nautilus did just that, embarking on a journey of nearly 1,600 kilometres (1,000 miles) underneath the Arctic ice cap.

But the Arctic is much larger than the North Pole! It stretches to 16.5 million square kilometres) and it includes parts of Canada, the United States, Finland, Sweden, Iceland, Russia and Greenland. Even so, most of the Arctic – about 14 million square kilometres – is made up of the Arctic Ocean, which is the smallest ocean in the world! The water freezes during winter, and there's a layer of ice covering throughout the year.

So is it really cold? Absolutely! If you ever travel to the Arctic, you will definitely need to wrap up warm. The average winter temperature is -40C and it once dropped as low as -70C in Greenland in 1991. But even though 84 per cent of Greenland's surface is covered in ice, the whole Arctic area – known as the Arctic Circle – has many features such as snowy mountains, icebergs, fjords and glaciers.

In fact, the glaciers and icebergs actually make up 20 per cent of the world's freshwater, and the area is very important because it helps to keep the planet's climate stable and cool. The Arctic also plays home to lots of natural resources, such as oil and natural gas, as well as copper, nickle and iron ore. There are no tall trees, though, just smaller ones such as birches and willows, along with grasses and mosses.

STATS

POPULATION: 4 million
LANGUAGES: Russian, English, Finnish, Scandinavian as well as between 40 and 90 indigenous languages
LARGEST CITIES:
1. Murmansk, Russia
2. Norilsk, Russia
3. Tromsø, Norway
4. Vorkuta, Russia
5. Apatity, Russia
SIZE: 16.5 million km^2

MURMANSK, RUSSIA

 HOW YOU PRONOUNCE MY NAME   MUH-MANSK

Just north of the Arctic Circle, this port city has a population of 307,000. There are two museums and three theatres.

76

NORILSK, RUSSIA

HOW YOU PRONOUNCE MY NAME NO-RUHLSH

This city is one of the most remote in the world, but it sits on lots of nickel, so it's a key centre for mining.

LOTS OF FISH!

HOW YOU PRONOUNCE MY NAME FI-SH

One of the main sources of food in the Arctic is fish. There are lots of salmon, cod, halibut, trout, eel and even sharks in the Arctic Ocean.

POLAR BEARS

HOW YOU PRONOUNCE MY NAME PO-LA BEAR

Polar bears are predatory marine mammals who love to swim in the icy waters as they move between pieces of ice.

ARCTIC CROSSWORD

Can you guess the names of these animals and complete the crossword? But watch out: there's an odd one out that doesn't belong in the Arctic. Fill their name in yellow.

Even though the Arctic is very cold, more than 4 million people call it their home. Around 40 ethnic groups live there, including the Inuits, Aleut, Yupik and Sami people, and their lives are very different to your life. They eat a diet that is high in fat because it is much harder to find fruit and vegetables. They also eat a lot of fish, which provides them with oil and omega-3s that keep their hearts healthy.

Many populations who have lived in the Arctic for thousands of years have adapted to the harsh climate. They are referred to as the indigenous people and they are physically well-built, with nasal passages that have narrowed so that the freezing air is more quickly warmed. Most people live in cities with fewer staying in the iciest areas. But they live in modern homes, maintain their traditions and share the land and sea with 75 species of mammals, 16 live under the ice or on top of it.

Of these wonderful animals, the biggest are the polar bears. You will also find arctic foxes, walruses, leopard seals and strangle-looking whales called narwhals, which have long tusks. Those living closest to the North Pole will be plunged into darkness for six months between September and March. They will be lit by ongoing daylight between April and August – it's light for 24 hours on 21 June and totally dark all day on 21 December.

Yet the environment is being threatened by climate change. Rising temperatures mean the ice cover is getting smaller and scientists believe that, by 2100, most of the Arctic sea ice will melt every Summer. As well as affecting the weather around the world, it will reduce the amount of space for people and animals to live. World leaders continue to discuss ways of slowing down the melting of the ice cap.

INUIT PEOPLE

 HOW YOU PRONOUNCE MY NAME IN-U-IT

The Inuit people live in the far north of Canada, Alaska and Greenland. They are perhaps best known for building amazing homes out of snow. These are known as igloos!

BEERENBERG, JAN MAYEN

 HOW YOU PRONOUNCE MY NAME BEER-EN-BURG

Beerenberg is a volcano that's 2,277 metres (7,470 feet) high. It last erupted in 1985, belching out seven cubic metres (24 cubic feet) of lava!

FIND THE IGLOO!

Igloos are dome-shaped shelters made from blocks of snow. Able to fit as many as 20 people, they trap body heat to warm the interior. Most of the snow and ice is trapped air and this acts as an insulator. Can you help this cold Inuit man find warmth in his igloo?

1
2
3

SNOWY OWL

HOW YOU PRONOUNCE MY NAME S-NO-WEE OW-EL

This beautiful bird is native to the Arctic region and they use their amazing hearing to sense their prey under the snow.

RUSSIAN SETTLERS

HOW YOU PRONOUNCE MY NAME RU-SHA

About 12.5 per cent of the Arctic population is indigenous peoples, but 2 million are Russian. Russia is the largest Arctic country.

NY-ÅLESUND, SVALBARD

HOW YOU PRONOUNCE MY NAME NEW ALL-SUN

The world's northernmost research station. It's used all year round by scientists studying physics, marine biology and more.

TROMSØ, NORWAY

HOW YOU PRONOUNCE MY NAME TRUM-SUH

A great place to see the northern lights – natural waves of light caused by electrons colliding with nitrogen and oxygen in the Earth's atmosphere.

ANTARCTICA

Antarctica is the world's southernmost continent. It's also the coldest, windiest, highest and driest continent, so it's perhaps no surprise that it's also the least populated. No one lives here all year round, and no one ever has.

Like the Arctic, Antarctica is an icy desert and dark six months of the year because it sits on the Earth's axis. But the average winter temperature is -60°C at the South Pole versus -40°C at the North Pole, and it remains subzero even in the summer months. Part of the reason why the frozen continent is so much colder is that it's surrounded by the Southern Ocean. This stormy sea blasts the land with frigid, hurricane-force winds. The continent is also covered in massive ice sheets and mountains, so the land has an average elevation of 2.3 km, and the higher you go, the colder it gets.

All of this means it's too cold to survive here without specialist clothes and equipment. You also can't grow crops, and it can be very dangerous trying to reach Antarctica by ship because of the icebergs. But perhaps because Antarctica is too hostile to make a permanent home, everyone is welcome. In 1958, countries made an agreement – or treaty – that no one can own or control the continent. Instead, it's a place of peace, international cooperation and shared discovery.

Every year, around 5,000 scientists from around the world come here for a few weeks or months. They live and work in 70 research stations scattered across the continent. Some watch the wildlife, including several species of penguins, seals and whales, while others explore the landscape and analyse the ice. A few even study outer space using a special telescope built at the South Pole. Then, when the scientists leave, they all share their findings, so everyone can benefit.

MCMURDO STATION

HOW YOU PRONOUNCE MY NAME MUHK-MUH-DOW STAY-SHN

Antarctica's largest base can house more than 1,250 people. It also has a harbour, three airfields and even a chapel.

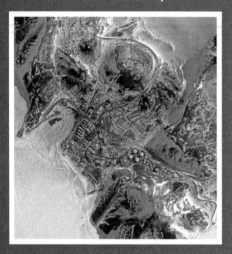

VOSTOK STATION

HOW YOU PRONOUNCE MY NAME VO-STOK STAY-SHN

This inland Russian station in the east of Antarctica once recorded the world's coldest temperature: -89.2°C

PORT LOCKROY

HOW YOU PRONOUNCE MY NAME PAWT LOK-ROY

Want to send a postcard home? Head to this British outpost that doubles as a post office. It can take months for letters to arrive from here though.

MOUNT EREBUS

HOW YOU PRONOUNCE MY NAME MOWNT EH-RUH-BUHS

The world's southernmost volcano erupts ten times a day and is crowned with a bubbling lava lake.

CEREMONIAL SOUTH POLE

HOW YOU PRONOUNCE MY NAME SEH-RUH-MOW-NEE-UHL

There are very few landmarks here, but this striped pole ringed by flags celebrates the signing of the Antarctic Treaty.

EMPEROR PENGUIN

HOW YOU PRONOUNCE MY NAME EM-PUH-RUH PENG-GWN

The largest penguin species live together in colonies of hundreds and even thousands, both on the ice and fishing in the frigid waters.

RACE TO THE POLE

Can you help Norwegian explorer Roald Amundsen become the first person to reach the South Pole in 1911?

STATS

POPULATION: 1,000-5,000
LANGUAGES: 24
LARGEST CITIES: None
SIZE: 14.2 million km²

END OF THE CHAPTER: THE WORLD

Everyone is slightly different. As individuals, we have our own thoughts, feelings and personalities. But we also have things in common with other people. We speak the same language, eat the same food, follow similar fashions in how we dress and come together to celebrate the same things.

The ways people live together is called a culture. With nearly 8 billion people around the world, there are thousands of cultures.

While continents are landmasses divided by oceans, we also sort them by shared cultural identity. This includes describing Europe and Asia differently, even though there isn't a physical border between them. On the other hand, Oceania is grouped together because of what their people have in common, despite being made up of lots of different islands.

There are also a lot of cultural differences within continents. For instance, the east and west of North America are very different from each other, as are the north and south. Countries – even large cities – can also be home to more than one culture. But no people or place exists solely on its own. You can see this in regions like Central America and the Middle East, which combine influences from different parts of the world. Travel and global trade also help share ideas far and wide so that cultures change over time.

WHAT HAVE YOU LEARNED?

Fill in the blanks with the supplied words to complete the ten sentences.

1 ....IS EQUALLY SPLIT BETWEEN THE NORTHERN AND SOUTHERN HEMISPHERES AND HAS MORE COUNTRIES THAN ANY OTHER CONTINENT.

2 NIAGARA FALLS BETWEEN THE .... AND .... AND IS ONE OF THE LARGEST WATERFALLS IN THE WORLD.

3 THE LARGEST COUNTRY IN ....IS RUSSIA. OTHER COUNTRIES INCLUDE ITALY, DENMARK AND POLAND.

4 ....IS THE WORLD'S LARGEST CONTINENT AND HOME TO THE TWO COUNTRIES WITH THE MOST PEOPLE: .... AND ....

5 THE ....IS AN ICY OCEAN SURROUNDED BY LAND, WHILE .... IS A FROZEN CONTINENT SURROUNDED BY WATER.

6 THE ....IS A REGION AROUND THE SOUTH-EASTERN SHORES OF THE... .... SEA, WHERE THE CONTINENTS OF EUROPE, ASIA AND AFRICA MEET.

7 THE PANAMA CANAL IN .... AMERICA OFFERS SHIPS A SHORTCUT FROM THE .... TO THE ATLANTIC.

8 THE MOST COMMON... LANGUAGES IN.. ....AMERICA ARE SPANISH AND... ....

9 ....IS THE CAPITAL OF INDONESIA AND THE LARGEST CITY IN SOUTHEAST ASIA.

10 .... IS MADE UP OF AUSTRALIA, ..., ... AND MANY OTHER ISLANDS.

INDIA   PACIFIC
CHINA   MIDDLE EAST
AFRICA   CANADA
PAPUA NEW GUINEA
OCEANIA
CENTRAL

MEDITERRANEAN
JAKARTA   ANTARCTICA
ARCTIC   EUROPE
ASIA   NEW ZEALAND
USA   SOUTH
PORTUGUESE

ANSWERS: 1. Africa, 2. USA, Canada, 3. Europe, 4. Asia, India, China, 5. Arctic, Antarctica, 6. Middle East, Mediterranean, 7. Central, Pacific, 8. South, Portuguese, 9. Jakarta, 10. Oceania, Papua New Guinea, New Zealand.

© Getty

WORLD PUZZLES

MARK THE MAP

Can you name all seven continents?

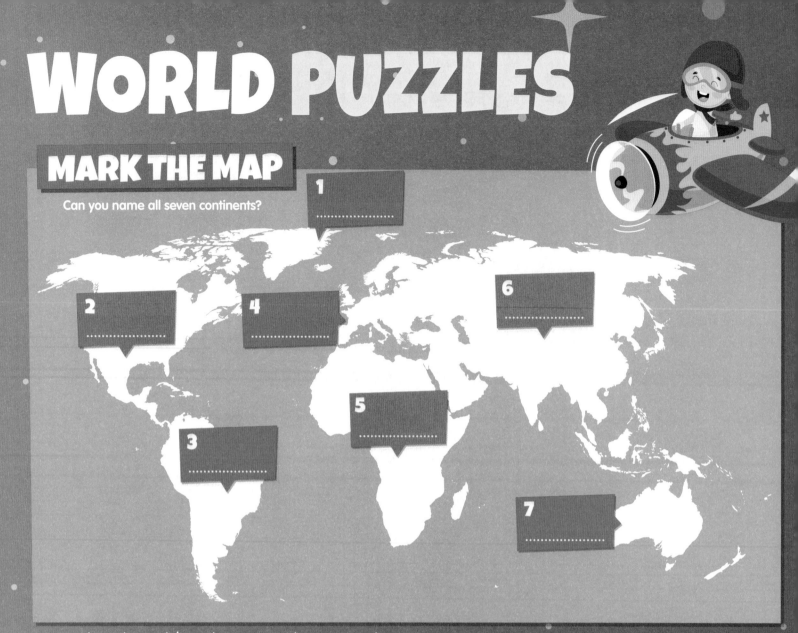

TROPIC CHALLENGE

Unscramble these words to spell out the names
of major lines of latitude and longitude

1 **RICCNAPO**

2 **CERNAC**

3 **MERMAID PINIER**

4 **ARTOQUE**

5 **ETON ROLPH**

6 **HELOT SOUP**

SAMBA DANCER DOT-TO-DOT

Get this performer ready for the Rio Carnival by joining the dots and colouring in their costume – the brighter the better!

DESTINATION EUROPE

Draw and colour in a poster to attract tourists to visit Europe. So visitors know what they can expect to see, include at least three landmarks.

MATCH THE MONUMENTS

Can you match these national landmarks with the countries they belong to?

EIFFEL TOWER

SYDNEY OPERA HOUSE

MOUNT RUSHMORE

GREAT SPHINX OF GIZA

AUSTRALIA

EGYPT

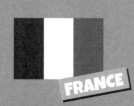

FRANCE

UNITED STATES OF AMERICA

SPOT THE SERENGENTI SNEAK

Which one of these animals doesn't live on the African savannah?

CHEETAH

ZEBRA

WARTHOG

OSTRICH

BEAVER

ANSWER: Beaver

WORLDWIDE WORD FIT

You've learnt lots of place names that you need to know to be a geography genius in this chapter. Fit these important ones into the grid below.

FOUR LETTERS
Doha
Lima
Nuuk

FIVE LETTERS
Dubai
Petra
Tokyo
Uluru

SIX LETTERS
Amazon
Berlin
Havana
London
Madrid
Tehran

SEVEN LETTERS
Bangkok
Beijing
Caracas
Jakarta
New York
Toronto

EIGHT LETTERS
Auckland
Brussels
Canberra
New Delhi
Svalbard

NINE LETTERS
Acropolis
Jerusalem

TEN LETTERS
Mexico City
Buenos Aires

ELEVEN LETTERS
Machu Picchu
Panama Canal

EXPLORE THE WORLD AROUND YOU

Now you've read all about the big wide world, are you ready to discover it for yourself? Over the next few pages, we've included loads of exciting activities, experiments and investigations for you to carry out and learn about where you live.

Geographers call this 'fieldwork', but you don't have to do it in a field and it doesn't have to be hard work. It's about exploring a place, asking questions about it and trying to find out the answers. It's thanks to fieldwork that we have such amazing maps and better understand different cultures. It's also how we know climate change is impacting the planet – and what we can do to stop it.

You can do all of the activities in this book by yourself or with friends. Once you've done that, why not carry out your own fieldwork? All you need to do is come up with a question (for instance, how many insects are in your garden), work out how you can answer it and what tools you'll need (perhaps look under rocks with a magnifying glass), and then go outside and do it!

Just remember, geographers always try to stay safe – whether they're up a mountain, in the lab or carrying out surveys on the street. With this in mind, always wear the right clothing to protect yourself, and stay near your adult.

SPOT THE DIFFERENCE

Can you spot seven differences from the two pictures below?

MAKE AND LEARN

DESIGN YOUR OWN FLAG

WHAT YOU'LL NEED

- Six A4 sheets of paper
- Sticky tape
- Scissors
- Coloured pens or crayons
- This book

INSTRUCTIONS

1. Roll two sheets of paper into tubes. Make sure you roll each one tightly and use sticky tape to secure them.
2. Slot the end of one tube into the other to make one long tube, then fasten them with sticky tape.
3. Lay the four other sheets of paper out flat on the table. Line them up so that they form one big rectangle, then tape them together.
4. Look through this book to get ideas for what shapes and colours to decorate your flag with.
5. Turn your extra large sheet over so the sticky tape is on the back, then decorate your flag with your coloured pens or crayons.
6. When you're finished, tape the long tube to the back of your flag. This will act as a flagpole. Make sure that it's attached securely so it won't fall apart when you wave it.

WHAT HAVE YOU LEARNED?

Every flag looks different, so you can easily tell who it belongs to. They also often only feature very simple shapes, like stars or stripes, so you can see them at a distance. But sometimes this symbol will be very meaningful to its people, such as the star-and-crescent symbol that appears on many Muslim countries flags. Flags also tend to use no more than three colours.

BE CAREFUL!

Only use the surgical spirit with windows open and don't leave the bottle open.

MAKE YOUR OWN THERMOMETER

WHAT YOU'LL NEED

- Clear plastic drinking straw
- Ruler
- Fine-tipped permanent marker
- Clean narrow-necked plastic bottle with lid
- ¼ cup of water
- ¼ cup of surgical spirit
- Tablespoon of cooking oil
- A few drops of food colouring
- Modelling clay

INSTRUCTIONS

1. Add the food colouring, water, surgical spirit and oil into the bottle and mix them together.
2. Draw a line with the permanent marker every half centimetre on the straw from top to bottom.
3. Mould the clay into a ball and push it flat. Then use your straw to pierce a hole through the middle.
4. Remove any clay clogging the straw, then put it back through the hole, and seal the clay over the bottle's neck.
5. Put the end of the straw in the liquid, but don't let it touch the bottom of the bottom. Most it will stick out the top.
6. Put the thermometer in the fridge and then outside and see how the liquid level differs.

WHAT HAVE YOU LEARNED?

The mixture moves up the straw when it gets warm, as heat makes the mixture fill up a slightly larger space. It goes down as the cold makes the mixture condense, so you can use it to track how much the temperature outside changes each day. For the best results, try to record your measurements at the same time every day.

MAKE A PAPIER-MÂCHÉ GLOBE

WHAT YOU'LL NEED

- A round balloon
- Newspaper
- Four cups of water
- One cup of flour
- ½ cup of resin glue powder
- Cling film
- Acrylic paint
- and painttbrush
- Saucepan
- Medium-sized container with lid
- Bowl
- Spoon
- This book

INSTRUCTIONS

1. Blow up your balloon so that it's big and round, then tie a knot in the end.

2. Tear your newspaper into strips, around 15cm long and 3cm wide. You'll need a lot of strips, so tear up several pages.

3. Pour three cups of water into the saucepan, then ask your adult assistant to bring it to the boil.

4. While the water is boiling, combine the cup of flour with the resin glue power in your container. Then add the last couple of water and stir it with your spoon to remove any lumps.

5. Once the saucepan is boiling, stir in the flour mixture. Boil it until it turns clear and smooth, then remove it from the heat. Once this paste is cool enough to work with, pour it back into your container.

6. Dip one newspaper strip into the paste until it's completely covered. Then gently run it through your fingers to squeeze off any excess paste, being careful not to tear it.

7. Stick the newspaper strip onto the balloon and smooth it down with your fingers.

8. Repeat steps six and seven, making sure the strips overlap and run in different directions.

9. Once the balloon is covered in a layer of strips, let it dry. This can take up to 24 hours. Meanwhile, put your lid on your container of paste and store it in the fridge.

10. When the first layer is dry, apply a second layer of newspaper strips in the same as the first. Then let it dry again, before adding a third and final layer.

11. Once your third layer of paper mache is dry, it's time to paint your globe. Use the maps in this book as a guide to the shape of the continents.

WHAT HAVE YOU LEARNED?

You'll discover how two-dimensional maps distort our idea of how Earth's curved surface really looks. For instance, North and South America appear at opposite ends to Australia and Asia on a flat page. But you can see that you can cross the Pacific directly from Los Angeles to Tokyo on your globe. Antarctica may also look smaller.

BE CAREFUL!

Don't boil water on your own. Ask an adult to help you.

© Getty Images

BUILD A WIND VANE

WHAT YOU'LL NEED

- A small plastic bottle
- Two A3 sheets of card
- A cork
- 200ml of sand
- Pen top
- Knitting needle
- Matchsticks
- Ruler
- Blu Tack
- Glue
- Scissors

INSTRUCTIONS

1. Draw the outline of 25cm long arrow on the card, making sure the arrow point is a little bigger than the tail end, then cut it out.
2. Make another arrow by tracing the first one and then cut it out.
3. Place the pen top between the arrows in the centre and glue together.
4. While that's drying, push four matchsticks into the long edge of the cork at right angles to each other.
5. Cut out four small squares of card and label with the main points of the compass: N, E, S, W. Attach these to the end of each matchstick with Blu Tack.
6. Fill the bottle with sand.
7. Push the knitting needle into the cork and push the cork in the top of the bottle. Now, balance the wind vane on top of the needle.
8. Choose an open area outside to place your wind vane. Use a compass to point the N label on the bottle towards North.

WHAT HAVE YOU LEARNED?

The arrow will always shows the direction the wind is blowing from. Record the wind for a week in a journal to see what direction it blows from and how the weather changes. When you're making your notes, be aware that winds are named after the direction they come from. For example, wind blowing from west to east is called westerly.

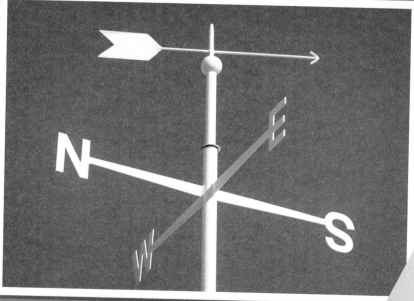

FIND YOUR BIRTHDAY COORDINATES

WHAT YOU'LL NEED

- A world map
- This book

INSTRUCTIONS

1. Use the month for latitude and day for longitude. For example, if your birthday is 28 September, your coordinates could be 28°N, 9°E.
2. Find out where these coordinates lead on a map. The latitude will be listed from top to bottom on the grid, while longitude will run from left to right.
3. Use this book to find out more about the country your birthday coordinates are in. What would it be like to have a party there?

WHAT HAVE YOU LEARNED?

Congratulations, and not just because you now know your birthday coordinates. You also now know how to plot coordinates on map, which is a very useful skill. Want to give it another go? Try reversing your coordinates to see where they lead, or use south latitude and west longitude instead of north and east.

CREATE YOUR OWN COMPASS

WHAT YOU'LL NEED

- Bowl
- Water bottle cap
- Water
- Paper clip
- Magnet
- Enamel paint or nail polish

INSTRUCTIONS

1. Straighten a paperclip and mark one end with a dab of enamel paint or nail polish.
2. Stroke the paperclip with the south pole of the magnet from the unmarked end to the marked end 50 times. Make sure you pull the magnet away from the paperclip between strokes.
3. Fill your bowl with water, then place the bottle cap in it so that it floats.
4. Place the paperclip on the bottlecap and watch it rotate. The painted tip will point towards the magnetic north.

WHAT HAVE YOU LEARNED?

Compass needles are affected by Earth's magnetic field. One end points towards magnetic north and the other end points south. You can make sure your compass works correctly if the end you didn't paint points towards the sun at midday, which is when it sits in the southern part of the sky.

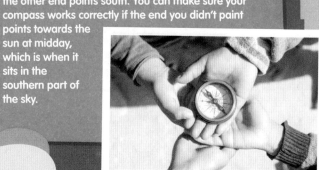

COUNTRIES QUIZ

WHAT YOU'LL NEED

- Alarm clock
- Paper
- Pen

INSTRUCTIONS

1. Set an alarm for five minutes.
2. Write down the names of as many countries as you can before the alarm goes off.
3. Add up how many you wrote down.

WHAT HAVE YOU LEARNED?

If you scored under 50, that's pretty good in such a short amount of time. More than 50? You're clearly a Future Genius. Over 100? You're so smart, you should have written this book! To improve your score, flick back through this book and try to memorise as many countries as you can, then try again.

EXCITING EXPERIMENTS

SEE HOW FOLD MOUNTAINS FORM

WHAT YOU'LL NEED

- Several different-coloured towels
- Two boxes
- A friend

INSTRUCTIONS

1 Fold each towel in half lengthways and stack them on top of the other. Imagine that these are the different layers of Earth's surface.

2 Put a box at either end of the stack of towels. These are going to act like tectonic plates.

3 Choose a box each and kneel behind them. Count to three, then push the boxes towards each other.

WHAT HAVE YOU LEARNED?

Did you see how the towels folded and parts were pushed upwards? The movement of tectonic plates can do the same thing, forcing the land above to buckle. This is one of the ways mountains form, including many of the world's biggest ranges. This includes the Himalayas, Alps, Andes and Rockies.

POLAR BEARS ON THIN ICE

WHAT YOU'LL NEED

- Two plastic trays or food containers
- Water
- Ice
- Small polar bear toys or modelling clay
- Spoon

INSTRUCTIONS

1 Pour about two centimetres of water into one of the containers and put it in the freezer.

2 If you're using modelling clay, sculpt a pair of polar bears and leave them to dry.

3 Once the ice is frozen solid, drop the container onto a worktop or jab the ice with the handle of a spoon to break it into large pieces.

4 Pour a couple of centimetres of cold water into the other container and add your ice.

5 Balance your polar bears on the ice. Notice how much space they have, and how close together the pieces of ice are.

6 Carefully pour in some room-temperature or lukewarm water. You can sit and watch what happens to the ice, or leave it and check back after ten minutes.

WHAT HAVE YOU LEARNED?

Sadly, this is really what's happening to the sea ice in the Arctic. Polar bears and other Arctic animals use the ice for hunting, breeding and resting. As the temperature of the ocean rises, the ice melts quicker and quicker, leaving them with less sea ice and greater distances to travel between the ice that's left.

SNOWSTORM IN A JAR

WHAT YOU'LL NEED

- Baby oil
- White paint
- Blue food colouring (optional)
- Alka-Seltzer tablet
- Water
- Teaspoon

INSTRUCTIONS

1 Pour water into the jar until it's about a quarter full, then stir in a teaspoon of white paint so it looks like milk.

2 Fill the rest of the jar with baby oil. Add a drop of blue food colouring if you'd like. Let the paint mixture settle on the bottom.

3 Break up an Alka-Seltzer tablet and drop the pieces into the jar one at a time.

WHAT HAVE YOU LEARNED?

Did you see how the Alkta-Seltzer reacts with the water and creates bubbles that push the paint mixture upwards? For the animals of the tundra, wind whips the snow up. Imagine trying to find food with all that whooshing past your face.

MAKE AN ERUPTING VOLCANO

BE CAREFUL!
Stand back when watching the eruption to make sure you don't get any in your eyes.

WHAT YOU'LL NEED

- Two A3 sheets of card
- A small plastic bottle
- ½ cup of vinegar
- 1 tbsp baking soda
- 1 tbsp washing-up liquid
- 1 tbsp red food colouring
- Small bowl
- Cup
- Pencil
- Scissors
- Sticky tape
- Paint and paintbrushes

INSTRUCTIONS

1 Place your bottle upside down in the centre of a sheet of card and draw a small circle around the neck with your pencil.

2 Cut a straight line through the card to the middle of the circle and cut it out.

3 Make a cone shape by overlapping the two sides of the card. Tape this into place, leaving a hole where you cut out the circle. Cut around the base of the cone so that it sits flat, but make sure that it's still taller than your bottle.

4 Place the cone over the bottle. Tape the top of the paper cone to the neck of the bottle to hold it in place. Tape the base of the cone to the other sheet of card.

5 Use paint to decorate the cone and make it look like a volcano.

6 While the paint is drying, combine the baking soda and washing-up liquid in your bowl. Add the water and mix thoroughly. Pour this mixture into your volcano.

7 In a cup, mix together the vinegar and food colouring.

8 When you're ready, pour the vinegar into the bottle with the baking soda. Wait for it to erupt and watch how the lava flows.

WHAT HAVE YOU LEARNED?

This model volcano erupts because combining the baking soda and vinegar produces carbon dioxide gas, which makes the mixture rise and flow out of the top. Real volcanic eruptions are caused by the shifting tectonic plates forcing magma to the surface, rather than a chemical reaction. But gases – including carbon dioxide – do build up as part of the process, which helps give eruptions their explosive energy. You can see evidence of gas bubbles in volcanic rocks like pumice and scoria, which are full of holes.

FIELDWORK FUN

MAP WHERE YOU LIVE

WHAT YOU'LL NEED

- A4 sheet of paper
- Colouring pencils
- Ruler

INSTRUCTIONS

1. Start by drawing your house in the centre of the map.
2. Next, draw your street and any surrounding roads. Decide whether you want to label them with their names.
3. Add any local landmarks that help you find your way home. This could be a statue, a large tree in a neighbour's garden, a friend's house or a particular shop.
4. Finally, draw a grid on your map using your ruler to create very straight lines crisscrossing vertically and horizontally. Then number each of these lines so that you can give coordinates of exactly where to find your house.

WHAT HAVE YOU LEARNED?

A map is only a two-dimensional representation of a place, so you often have to think as much about what information you're going to leave out as you do about what you're going to include to make it easy to follow. To see how well your map works, why not hide treasure somewhere in your local area, mark the location with an X on your map, and see if a friend can find it?

STUDY YOUR STREET

WHAT YOU'LL NEED

- Notebook
- Pen
- Camera

INSTRUCTIONS

1. Explore your local neighbourhood and make notes on what you see. For instance, what sort of shops are there? Are many people wearing hats? How many people are riding bikes rather than driving cars?
2. Use your camera to take pictures to help you remember what you saw.
3. When you get home, look through your notes and photos and think about what it tells you about where you live.

WHAT HAVE YOU LEARNED?

Exploring isn't just about going to far-off places; you can learn a lot by carrying out fieldwork on your doorstep. For instance, the number of bikes you see might tell how safe your roads are for cyclists, while the number of people wearing hats might tell you what your climate is like. Once you've had some practice, consider what question you want to answer before you carry out a field study.

NAVIGATE USING NATURE

WHAT YOU'LL NEED

- Two large sticks
- Four rocks

INSTRUCTIONS

1. Put a stick in the ground in a flat, sunny spot.
2. Place a rock at the tip of the stick's shadow, then wait 20 minutes.
3. As the sun moves across the sky, the shadow will have also moved. Mark its position with another rock.
4. Repeat this every 20 minutes until you've laid a line of four rocks.
5. Now, lay your second stick on the ground at a right angle to your rocks, pointing away from the shadow-making stick.
6. You now have a sun compass to guide you. The stick on the ground points straight north (if you're in the northern hemisphere), while your stones from left to right mark west and east.

WHAT HAVE YOU LEARNED?

The sun moves east to west, but shadows are like reflections in the mirror, so each new shadow marker will be to the east of the previous marker. With this survival skill, you can always find your way when exploring. For best results, you should do it before noon when the sun is still at an angle, rather than directly overhead.

WHERE DOES YOUR FOOD COME FROM?

WHAT YOU'LL NEED

- A recipe book or product packaging
- Laptop, desktop computer or smart device
- This website: gernot-katzers-spice-pages.com/engl/spice_geo.html
- This book

INSTRUCTIONS

1. Get the recipe for your favourite family food and find out what herbs and spices it contains. If this is homemade, the recipe might be written down in a book. If the food is from a shop, check the ingredients listed on the packaging.
2. Go to the website on your device and find the herbs and spices you're looking for among its long list.
3. Click on the herb or spice to learn more about it, including where it is grown.
4. Look up the countries or regions these ingredients are from and find out more about them.
5. Ask yourself, what kind of climates do these places have? Could you grow the same spices where you live? If not, why not?

WHAT HAVE YOU LEARNED?

The food we eat is often made from ingredients that come from all over the world. Often this is because ingredients need to be grown in particular climates. It can also be because other countries have more space to grow food, are particularly efficient at growing it, or the cost of production is cheaper.

KEEP A WEATHER DIARY

WHAT YOU'LL NEED

- A 2 ltr plastic bottles
- Thermometer
- Compass
- Wind vane
- Scissors
- Notebook
- Pencils and pens

INSTRUCTIONS

1. Make a rain gauge by cutting the top off your bottle. Turn this upside down and put it back on the bottle to act as a funnel. Then mark intervals every centimetre on the bottle with a pen.
2. Choose a place to put your rain gauge that you can visit regularly, such as your garden, balcony or front door steps.
3. At the same time every day, check how high the water level has reached in your rain gauge, record it in your notebook and then empty out the water.
4. Next, record the temperature with your thermometer and the wind direction with your vane.
5. You could also record how many clouds you can see and what they look like. Are they fluffy and white or big and grey?

WHAT HAVE YOU LEARNED?

By keeping detailed records of your weather measurements and observations, you can build up a picture of what your local weather is like and track the changes in the season. After a while, you can start to analyse the results. Which month had the most varied weather? Was the summer as sunny as you expected? What was the average temperature during winter?

GO ON A GEOCACHE TREASURE HUNT

WHAT YOU'LL NEED

- Laptop, desktop computer or smart device
- This website: geocaching.com
- Pen

INSTRUCTIONS

1. Go to the website, or download the free Geocaching app and create a free account.
2. Look up where you live, see what geocaches are listed nearby and choose one.
3. If you have the app, it will direct you to where to find the cache. Alternatively, you can print out a map to follow. But if you do that, make sure you also write down any 'hints' that other players have left online.
4. Geocaches are hidden in public places, so you might have to look around a bit. Sometimes you'll have to search for clues in several locations to help you find the final container.
5. When you find it, sign your username in the geocache's logbook to record that you were there.
6. Place the geocache back where you found it so that other people can enjoy it too.

WHAT HAVE YOU LEARNED?

There is a secret treasure hunt going on worldwide every single day. Geocaching is a great way to explore the great outdoors and test your map-reading skills. But it's not just limited to the countryside; in fact, there are many more caches to be found in towns and cities.

HOW NOISY IS YOUR NEIGHBOURHOOD?

WHAT YOU'LL NEED

- A smart device
- Decibel X app
- Notebook
- Pen

INSTRUCTIONS

1. Download the Decibel X sound meter app for free on either an iOS or Android device.
2. Choose somewhere to carry out your research, such as a street corner where a lot of cars drive by.
3. Use the app to scan your street and it'll give you a reading in decibels, which is the measurement of how loud noises are.
4. Take measurements at regular intervals and write down the readings along with the date and time in your notebook.
5. Once you've taken lots of measurements, add all your decibel readings together and then divide them by the number of readings you've taken. This will give you an average decibel level. For instance, the average of 1,2,3,3,4 and 5 is 18 divided by 6, which is 3.

WHAT HAVE YOU LEARNED?

If the average volume in your neighbourhood is above 70 decibels, it is higher than scientists recommend for shopping and traffic areas. But think about when you made your recordings, was it at a particular time of day when the roads were busy? Was there something going on that might have caused more noise than normal, such as building work? If so then you might need to do further research.

FUN FACTS ABOUT THE WORLD

2,600 KILOMETRES

The length of the Great Barrier Reef in Australia. Strewth!

267,570

Number of islands in Sweden – more than any other country

-97.7 DEGREES CELSIUS

EARTH'S LOWEST RECORDED TEMPERATURE, TAKEN IN ANTARCTICA IN 2018. BRR!

THE CENTRE OF THE EARTH IS HOTTER THAN THE SUN

AFRICA EXISTS IN ALL FOUR HEMISPHERES

4.64 BILLION

NUMBER OF PEOPLE IN ASIA – THAT'S 60% OF ALL HUMANS!

The world's longest mountain range, the mid-ocean ridge, is underwater

Damascus is the oldest city still inhabited today

DOMINICA   NICARAGUA

ONLY TWO COUNTRIES USE PURPLE IN THEIR FLAG